K9 SCENT TRAINING

K9 Professional Training Series

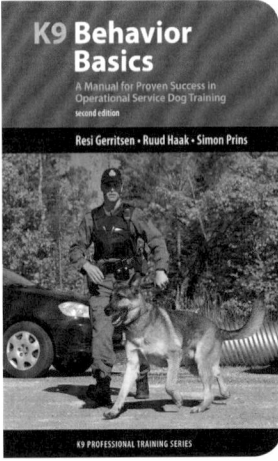
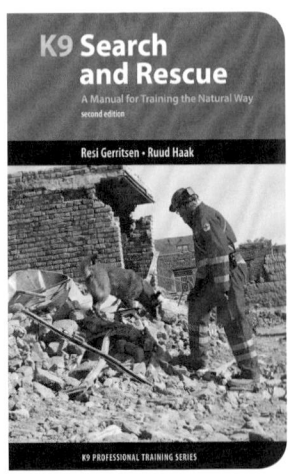

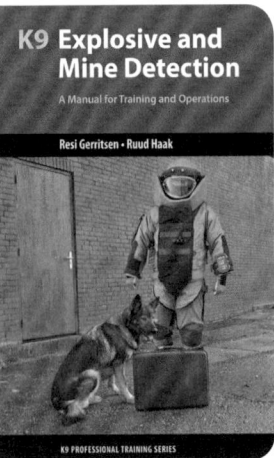

See the complete list at
dogtrainingpress.com

K9 SCENT TRAINING

A Manual for Training Your Identification, Tracking, and Detection Dog

Dr. Resi Gerritsen
Ruud Haak

K9 PROFESSIONAL TRAINING SERIES

An imprint of
Brush Education Inc.

Introduction

The way dogs experience the world differs from that of most humans in that olfaction replaces vision as the dominant modality of sensation. Knowing this, we have made and continue to make use of our four-legged friends' exceptional ability to perceive non-visual cues in order to supplement our own sensory capabilities. In some cases, such as hunting, people rely on dogs' innate patterns of behavior to achieve the desired results. In other situations, however, such as in detection of odors, dog handlers use conditioning techniques to train their dogs to work alongside and communicate with them.

For example, police dogs detect odor traces or substances. When committing a crime, an offender comes into direct contact with his victim or with objects. Consequently, he often leaves traces (fingerprints, footprints, marks left by objects). Crime-scene investigators throughout the world today give increasing importance to the physical changes to a crime scene made by scent prints. They also analyze traces of substances found at a scene, on a victim, or on an offender. Scientific progress in recent decades has led to a reduction in the amount of odorous substance investigators require for successful analysis. This in turn has led to the possibility of carrying out analyses on microtraces (microscopic amounts of substances). A human smell is a particular type of microtrace.

Based on our experience with tracker dogs, we believe that an offender can be identified by the particular smells he leaves behind at the crime scene. Each person has a distinctive smell; this has been proven by experience as well as by experiments using various apparatus. Mass spectrography has also been used to analyze and identify human odors.[1] The identification of offenders by analyzing traces of their odors has increased in importance as it has been scientifically proven that no two individuals smell alike.

All humans perspire. When it is hot, odor molecules from human perspiration disperse into the environment; this dispersal increases as the temperature increases. The human body seeks to maintain its average body temperature (98.6°F/37°C), and when it is hot, perspiring helps the body cool off. As well, when we experience fear, or undergo physical or emotional exertion, our body temperatures rise, which leads to increased perspiration and accompanying odor. We don't like to admit it, but we are sources of smells, and when we move about we leave behind odors. The entire human body emits smells. For example, when we walk across a room, odor molecules are released onto the floor and become attached to other objects we touch. Thus, despite any and all meticulous precautions he may take, an offender cannot avoid leaving traces of his specific smell at the scene of a crime. He can neither destroy secretions nor prevent them from forming.

Each dog's nose depends on its individual physical qualities, its training, and the frequency with which it is used. Even a dog with a natural talent for sniffing things out must be trained well in order to be able to identify odors correctly. Daily training, increasing in difficulty as the training period progresses, helps dogs develop conditioned reflexes. The sole aim of training a dog to identify odors is to teach him to make optimum use of his exceptional gifts in order to meet human needs.

A dog's ability to detect and, by inference, objectively identify odors depends on proper training techniques. If he doesn't regularly practice identifying smells under his handler's supervision, the dog will not be successful when he sets out to detect and identify odors. So, scent-detection dogs aren't ready for work unless they train regularly and systematically.

The dog's sex is an interesting factor when it comes to scent detection. It has long been known that females have a better sense of smell than males, so it might seem surprising that police dogs are almost exclusively males (hence the use of the masculine pronoun relative to dogs throughout this book). It seems that the presence of females, particularly when in heat, can upset males. In addition, a female's sense of smell decreases considerably when she is in heat, and her work is therefore not effective for a 16 to 24–day period every six months, and may even be affected weeks before and after this period. Most spayed (also called neutered or castrated) females, however, do not cause the same upset to males, nor do they experience periodic decreases in their sense of smell, and so their search work is consistent.

Training improves a dog's sensitivity to smells, enabling him to progressively detect fainter and fainter traces of odors. In this book, we have drawn up special training programs to this effect, and the overall effectiveness of the exercises has been demonstrated in practice. Drawing from our extensive experience in training our many service dogs the sorting, tracking, and detecting skills they need to find, for example, drugs or explosives, we have laid out here the specific exercises your dog needs to practice to become a scent-detection expert. In this book, we also tell you about the mistakes that can be made in different training programs, clearly justifying our method. Moreover, we insist that teaching a dog to track is the logical next step after teaching him how to sort odors.

And, of course, in this book you will find the necessary hints and tips that will help you help your dog learn. Following are the first three:

1. *Identification:* When sorting odors, always be aware of the so-called Clever Hans effect, by which a dog reacts

to minimal and often unconscious changes in posture or other small movements made by you, the handler, or others present, as soon as he approaches the matching odor. (You can read more about this subject in our book *K9 Fraud!*)
2. *Tracking:* If your dog has lost the track, try to find it again by approaching where you think it might be at an angle of 90°. Your dog's behavior will tell you if you are back on track again: if he crosses the track, he will turn left or right and will follow the track again.
3. *Detection:* Although it is not pleasant, always take a close look at dog waste bags. Several times we have found drugs in such bags, casually placed next to other poop bags or near garbage bins.

Identifying the odors you present to your dog is not a natural activity for him, and so he must be specially trained to do so. A dog does not identify a human smell just because it is there. A scent-detection dog does this for his handler and for the reward he gets in return. A dog's attachment to his handler is therefore the foundation of scent-detection training and the work that follows. Always remember that your behavior and skills as a handler have a profound influence on your dog. His accomplishments are the result of the tight bond he has with you, his two-legged partner.

—Dr. Resi Gerritsen and Ruud Haak

Disclaimer

While the contents of this book are based on substantial experience and expertise, working with dogs involves inherent risks, especially in dangerous settings and situations. Those using approaches described in this book do so entirely at their own risk and both the author and publisher disclaim any liability for any injuries or other damage that may be sustained.

1

Living in Different Worlds

Usually, dogs and people pay attention to different things in their environments. A lot of things we don't notice, or turn up our noses at (because they stink so much) are of great importance to dogs. As a dog handler, you have to understand this difference between what humans regard as important and what is vital to dogs in reading their surroundings. If you understand your dog's need to sniff certain things, you can better understand his behavior when he is searching for a scent during an exercise or at work.

The Human World versus the Dog World

The human world and that of dogs are incredibly different. German professor Dr. J. von Uexküll provides an apt description of these two spheres when he writes:

> A human and his dog walk together in a town. The handler passes a clothes shop and is very interested in the clothes displayed there, then he goes along to a jeweler's, where he looks at the rings and watches on show in the shop window. At last he stops at a bookstore, where he looks at books and magazines, which can satisfy his spiritual needs. He pays less attention to the butcher shop. Man and dog walk around a corner

The all-important iron pole located at the corner of the street, embellished by a bronze dog in Brussels, Belgium. Every male dog that passes a pole like this—or a fire hydrant, mailbox, street-light base, or any other number of like structures—makes a stop to deposit a more or less strong odor flag.

Only the cushions on chairs are interesting to him, because they are so very soft.

into a park and up a staircase to a terrace, where the man sits on a chair and looks at the nice flowerbeds around him.

The dog experiences the world totally differently when he goes out on this same walk with his owner. He passes the clothes shop; the things hanging in the shop window don't interest him. Clothes are only interesting when his owner or another person has worn them and they have absorbed body odor. The displays of watches and books also don't interest him—these represent nothing more than an unimportant mess of lines and surfaces that do not smell interesting. But the butcher shop says more to him. The odor of meat and sausages sparks his appetite and he wants to roll around in whatever is creating that rich odor of waste. Of utmost importance to him, however, is the stone on the street corner. How could his owner have just walked by it? Every male dog that has passed by the stone has planted an odor flag on it. The dog studies these very seriously, and only after he has added his own flag can he continue on the walk. The staircase to the terrace is like walking up a hill, and he doesn't really notice that the slope is interrupted by stairs. The rail of the staircase is unimportant, but the cushions on the chairs interest him. They lie there, so very soft. He sees nothing of the park's beauty, but the mouse emerging from a flowerbed sparks his interest immediately.[1]

DIFFERENT WORLDS

As you can see, dogs' interests are mostly limited to what is of direct and vital importance to them. Does your dog observe his reflection in the mirror on the wall of the living room? Does he take an interest in the table and cupboards, or does he simply walk around them? The plates on the table will, of course, attract him if they are filled with food. But does he ever notice the sky or the tops of the trees as anything other than a background to couple of flying ducks, or to a cat escaping into the trees? Does he note the singing of the birds? (His sense of hearing is excellent, after all.) Does he distinguish between the odors of different flowers? If you train him to do so, he will, but what about ordinarily?

Ordinarily, all of the things mentioned above exist outside your dog's sphere of interest. His world is not only different from ours but also much smaller.

PERCEPTION AND INTEREST

Dutch professor Dr. F.J.J. Buytendijk wrote about canine perception in his book *De Psychologie van den Hond (The Psychology of the Dog)*: "Mostly one imagines that perception with the sense organs is a passive process. In this way, sight perception should be the reception of light prickles on the retina; hearing decided by the vibrations on the eardrum; smelling because of particles of dust coming into the olfactory mucous membrane . . . . This opinion is not right!"[2]

What the dog perceives is not coincidental to his environment but depends largely on his interests; his perception is active, not passive. Sensory impressions affect dogs when they have a biological meaning: that is, when objects play an obvious role in a dog's life, he will pay attention to them. For example, the odor of other dogs is important, as is the sound of a barking dog or the sight of a cat crossing the street nearby.

The amount of attention a dog pays to a certain perception also depends on experience. A dog's reaction to the approach of a person or another animal he recognizes by odor or sound depends on what the dog knows of that person or other animal; his experience informs his perception and therefore his response.

Humans also have different perceptions based on interest. When a painter, a biologist, and an engineer walk through a landscape, for example, they each experience different things because of their different experiences, professional training, and interests. Similarly, a cow's main interests in a meadow will differ widely from those of a dog. The dog in the meadow will not be interested in examining different plants; the cow will not see the little mouse in the grass because she is too busy finding or eating her favorite vegetation. Each animal's field of interest correlates with its vital needs. Because of that, a single species may live in a world completely different from other species, even if they all live in the same habitat.

Training

When you train your dog, you give him the experience he needs to become interested in sensory input that an untrained dog might not notice. For instance, only highly trained dogs can locate drugs or explosives, or, as is the case with search-and-rescue (SAR) dogs, find people beneath piles of debris. These specially trained dogs have sometimes been called "super dogs," and some people have wrongly supposed they possess a special intelligence, sometimes even a kind of clairvoyance. SAR and scent-detection dogs are, however, just normal dogs whose already fine ability to perceive has been heightened by training.

The dog's nose is not the only thing a handler trains when teaching him the skills associated with scent detection. A dog's ability to perceive is also partly determined by his movements, after all. For instance, if you were blindfolded and a familiar object was placed in your hands, you would be able to recognize it by feeling its shape and texture. Similarly, when the dog moves his head, eyes, ears, and nose, he stimulates his own ability to perceive. If you want to find out more about the functions of your dog's olfaction, make sure you give him as much opportunity as possible to make all the movements he needs to make to augment sniffing.

Through training, your dog can become an expert in sniffing out specific substances, such as truffles.

It is illogical to think that tracking dogs use only their noses when searching and do not employ their eyes to look for changes in the terrain.

Some question whether or not the dog's ability to sense his surroundings is compromised if his senses are somehow compartmentalized. For example, we know that children understand the spoken word better when they are able to see the face of the speaker: the speaker's facial expressions, the shape of her mouth when forming words, the movement of her head—all help the child recognize the words spoken. Dogs, too, are used to combining sight and smell in their everyday lives; the combination of sounds, tastes, and textures, sensation of temperature, too, also helps dogs explore their environments. It makes no sense to suppose that tracking dogs only use their noses when searching and don't employ their eyes to look for changes or damage to the terrain.

TEMPERATURE AND PERCEPTION
Temperature plays an important role in the perception of odors. Warm substances give off more odor in cold surroundings than warm substances in hot surroundings. It is more difficult to find a cold article by its smell when the ambient temperature is low. Substances or articles that already give off recognizable odor under

normal circumstances smell stronger when they become warmer. Warm foods, as you know, smell much stronger than cold foods. As well, freezing a warm food, such as a steak, causes the smells emitting from it to decrease so that it hardly smells at all. Of course, the steak will still give off some recognizable smell when it is frozen; it releases a minute amount of odor into the air, which, when breathed in and warmed up in our noses, penetrates the olfactory epithelium and its odor receptors.

SENSING GREAT EVENTS

Scientists involved in the prediction of earthquakes have long known that dogs and other animals show a remarkable change in behavior before an earthquake happens. One night when doing research in the field, Don Stierman, a geologist at the University of California, couldn't sleep because of the continuous barking of dogs. During the day he had been with a colleague performing measurements in connection with two serious earthquakes that had taken place the day before in southern California. As they took their measurements that day, they noticed that light tremors, which they could measure with their equipment but not feel themselves, were preceded every time by a continuous barking of dogs. This confirmed the centuries-old results of studies made by researchers from Japan and China.[3]

Before the major earthquake that destroyed San Francisco in 1906, changing animal behavior was also observed and described in the official report of the American Commission of Investigation under the direction of A.C. Lawson:

> The night before the earthquake dogs were whining and barking almost continuously. Near Santa Rosa, about ten seconds before the very serious tremors began, a dog began to walk restlessly around in the house and then jumped out of the open window of the first floor. Other dogs also left their places before the earthquake or refused to go into certain houses, buildings or shops, even when their owner pressured

them strongly. During the earthquake there were dogs barking piteously and walking around anxiously with their tails between their legs. Other dogs were still walking aimlessly long after the earthquake. Similar behavior was also observed during the lighter aftershocks.[4]

This knowledge about dog behavior before, during, and after earthquakes is vital for search-and-rescue dog handlers. Dogs sense the dangers of collapsing buildings almost faultlessly. SAR dog handlers have to watch the behavior of their dogs constantly when they are working, and they must interpret that behavior correctly to reduce risks. A well-trained dog that refuses to go into a house because he senses danger is entirely different from a dog refusing to work. A well-trained SAR dog handler will, of course, know the difference and know how to evaluate the behavior of the dog.

A SMELLING ANIMAL

The dog is, above all, a smelling animal; olfaction delivers the greatest amount of input to him, and he will perceive the outside world through this sense before any other. Hearing is second most important, followed by sight. In humans, sight is the dominant sense. Most people arrange the articles in a room or the flowers in a garden in such a way that they can see them and find a way through them using their sense of sight. Dogs live primarily in a world of odor, so they generally perceive a room full of articles as a space filled with odor towers and large odor surfaces, which dictate how they will react to and orient themselves in the space.

Handlers must remember that dogs navigate the world on four legs, head close to the ground. We cannot really imagine the dog's sense of space, not even when we crawl around on our hands and knees. Humans simply have a different physique than dogs and because of that a different spatial sense. It is vital for handlers working with search dogs to understand as many differences between them and their dogs as possible before they begin training

Two noses—and worlds of difference.

or working; knowing how a dog perceives the world can make all the difference when it comes to assessing dog behavior.

The Underrated Sense

Humans' ability to smell is often underrated. Dutch Professor P. Vroon wrote this: "When people were asked which sense they would miss the most, sight was at the top of the list. The sense of smell takes a humble place. But that decision was taken a bit too quickly. The sense of smell is an old and important sense. We simply don't realize how much we are influenced by it."[5]

Olfactory dysfunction can lead to dangerous circumstances and be a reason for serious health problems. The sense of smell even plays a role in learning and memory. Dysosmia is the term generally used for olfaction dysfunction. The condition can take a variety of forms: anosmia, for example, is characterized by the inability to detect odors, and hyposmia is a milder form of anosmia exemplified by a decreased sensitivity to smell. All subconditions of dysosmia can affect the afflicted person's sense of taste, too, since the oral cavity and olfactory system are connected.

Most of our senses are connected to the brain via the nervous system. Eyes and ears, for example, send the information they have collected to different parts of the brain via neurons and synapses. The same is true for the senses of touch and taste. The olfactory system as an ancient organ of sense, however, is direct contact with that portion of the brain that is placed high in the nose. In addition to this direct smell-to-brain perception route, we perceive some odors when they enter our bloodstream via the nose. And we perceive other smells via the nervous system, which brings coded messages about smells to the limbic system of the brain, the structure that translates various stimuli so that we can express emotions appropriate to those stimuli.

Far from being irrelevant, what might seem to be the most insignificant smell prickles are actually indispensable. Those, for example, who lose the ability to smell after a knock on the head or as a result of certain viral infections not only experience diminished ability to taste but also are exposed to danger: perhaps they don't smell the scent of bad meat or discover a little late that the kitchen is ablaze. The limbic systems of those who have lost their sense of smell are also deprived of olfactory input, which can lead to depression and loss of sexual interest. Depression, in turn, can lead to other health complications, including a compromised immune system and resulting illnesses.

WITHOUT SMELL

In his book *The Man Who Mistook His Wife for a Hat*, neurologist Oliver Sacks describes a talented man who lost his ability to smell when he received a blow to his head. This was a serious shock for him. "My sense of smell?" he said. "I never thought about it. But when I lost it, it was as if I suddenly became blind. Life has lost a big part of its savor; you don't realize how much taste comes out of scent. You smell people, smell books, you smell the city and smell the spring—maybe not aware, but as a pattern of unconscious background for all the other stuff. My world was suddenly much, much poorer . . ."

His neurologists did not think he would recover. But suddenly, some months later, his beloved morning coffee, which had become tasteless, was beginning to taste again. Hesitant, he tried his pipe, which he hadn't touched for months, and there also he picked up a trace of the rich aroma he loved so much. He went back to his doctor. But after the doctor tested him carefully, using a double-blind technique, he said, "No, I am sorry, there is absolutely no way. You still have a total disability to smell. But it's crazy that you can 'smell' your pipe and your coffee again . . ."

What possibly happened is that only the olfactory system (not the brain stem) was damaged, and thus the man's recovered experiences of smell were the result of a powerful smell memory. In drinking his coffee, lighting up his pipe, actions associated with odor, he was able to unconsciously call the odors back, and with such an intensity that he thought he had recovered.[6]

WORDS FOR SMELLS AND ODOR INTENSITY

As you can see, the nose is an ancient and evolved organ of sense. On the one hand, we are able to recall or describe countless forms of items we experience every day. The hundreds of thousands of odors we can differentiate between have, on the other hand, few words to describe them. The words we do have in our vocabulary to describe odors rely on the names of the substances emitting the odors ("It stinks like benzene." "Your apartment smells of roses."). In many cases, we must make do with describing an odor as pleasant or unpleasant, or by way of hazy analogies ("This odor reminds me of . . .").

Even though we have not developed a complicated smell vocabulary, odors have a complicated effect on us. For example, the perception thresholds of light of different frequencies don't make a big difference to us: when we see red or green light, the intensity of the colors doesn't really affect us. However, the intensity of some odors, and the sensitivity we have to them, can be a thousand times greater than for others. It is not known why this is the case. We do know that we perceive odors faster if they represent potential or actual danger (an exception is carbon monoxide, which is odorless to us). This connection between threshold intensity and danger demonstrates that our sense of smell is directly related to survival. This is true for both humans and dogs.

Hearing, Sight, and Smell: The Trinity of Senses

The older animals in wild dog packs do everything they can to teach the young the basics of searching, not only for food to support the group but also to track down enemies in their territory. Hunting and establishing and maintaining a territory require a fine sense of hearing supported by olfaction.

A dog's ability to hear is much better than that of humans, who are really rather primitively equipped in this regard. The audible range for humans is 20 to 20,000 Hertz. Dogs, however, can hear frequencies from 40 to 60,000 Hertz, which is why the "soundless" (high-frequency) dog whistle can be heard by dogs but not by humans. As a result of his great hearing range, the dog can recognize the unique footsteps of his owner and even the specific engine murmur of his owner's car.

On the whole, humans see better than domestic dogs do, especially objects located a great distance away, although dogs do see sudden movements quicker than we do. The domestic dog's dull sense of sight may be attributed to his being a house pet, though, because wild canines have an excellent sense of vision, as Doctors R. and R. Menzel concluded in 1960.[7] The results of the research of Professor H. Stephan in 1954 already indicated this.[8] Stephan investigated the brains of wild animals and house pets and discovered that the auditory and visual areas of the cerebrum (where hearing and sight impressions come to awareness) in the brains of house pets were 40 per cent smaller than those of wild canines with brains of equal weight.

That said, our height allows us to have superior sight to any dog, wild or domestic. If you think about how low to the ground the dog is compared to an adult human, it makes sense that the dog would evolve to have such keen senses of hearing and smell. These senses are crucial to their ability to protect themselves in a world of danger.

What a dog perceives by scent often depends on his interests and training.

For our purposes, it is valuable to know Stephan's conclusion: unlike the auditory and visual rinds, the allocortex—much of which is used to process scent—is hardly smaller in domestic dogs in comparison to wild canines. He concludes that the dog's sense of smell was obviously less affected by domestication. This may be because the olfactory organ is an ancient and primitive one, existing in less-developed animals than dogs, and therefore less likely to be affected by a change of environment, such as what occurred during domestication.

The olfactory system is also developed in newborn puppies. Even when their eyes are still closed and their ears folded back, closing the hearing canal, they are able to find, by warmth and mainly by smell, their mother's nipples. Professor J. Bodingbauer posited that the speed with which a puppy could find that food source was equal to the sensitivity of his sense of smell.[9] Bodingbauer's observation may be worth keeping in mind when you select puppies to be trained as scent-detection dogs.

Remembering Odors

Most animals' memories associated with odors are very strong. Laying down memories related to smell starts earlier than most people think: animals remember odors from before birth. When in the uterus, animals learn the specific odor of the amniotic fluid they are suspended in. This was shown by letting newborn lambs and human babies choose between the odor of their own amniotic fluid and that of another, equally old, conspecific fluid. Both lambs and human babies prefer the smell of their own amniotic fluid, which shows that the amniotic fluid of different individuals smells differently and that animals in utero memorize this odor before birth.[10]

It follows, then, that smell memory can be manipulated. Researchers have done this by feeding pregnant rabbits and sheep different diets. It appeared that the young rabbits and lambs reacted differently to the diet of their mothers than to other food: another proof that memory for odor is formed prenatally. In the rabbit study, it was demonstrated that not only the behavior relative to the odor of the food was different, but also there were physical differences in the olfactory epithelium, which allowed for a stronger reaction to this odor.[11]

Dogs have a fine memory for odors. A dog will recognize the odor of his mother, and the mother will remember the odor of her young, even after two years.[12] Puppies memorize odors associated with their mothers particularly well. But dogs lay down smell memories well even when the odors are not associated with their mothers. Laboratory studies have shown that odors dogs have been trained to recognize are still fresh in their memories three months later, without additional training. There is evidence that they can remember odors for considerably longer than three months, too.[13]

ODOR AND MEMORY

It is essential that children are able to smell their mothers as soon as they are born for emotional development to progress normally. A baby, using her sense of smell, will react differently to clothes her mother is wearing than to another woman's clothing. As we age, we retain this ability to recognize other humans by their particular odors. In particular, almost everyone can differentiate between the genders by olfaction alone.

Our sense of smell also informs our emotions. For example, unfamiliar odors can cause children to feel homesick. A child who has access to a familiar smell—a cuddly toy or blanket—when away from home, however, may be able to avoid feeling glum. This same principle works with puppies, too. When you bring a new puppy home, make sure you also bring along a toy or piece of cloth that smells like the litter; the well-known smell of this little item will help put your puppy at ease in his new world of strange odors.

Even the lofty astronaut is not above the need for smells of home when out and about on long travels in an odorless environment. Researchers have tried to improve quality of life in space by providing astronauts with bottles containing familiar odors associated with good memories. In need of the scent of home? Just open this little bottle!

Everybody knows that odors not only bring back memories but also stir up memories of events long buried, even thought to be forgotten. There are cases of people who couldn't remember anything about their nursery school days until they sniffed a typical school odor and were able to recall images of the school, teachers, other children, and even specific games played or other events. This connection between odor and memory also may explain why a dog can recognize, often after many years, a previous owner.

2

Human Odor on Objects

An "odor" is that which stimulates the olfactory organ. According to Professor J. Bodingbauer, we use our noses and sense of smell to pick up on odors, and we translate what we smell into personal meanings, based on our own subjective realities.[1] The senses of smell and taste are both sensitive to chemicals in the environment around us. Odors, after all, have a chemical character; carried in gases in the air or in liquids, they exert their influence on our olfaction. When you smell an odor, you are in fact taking a gas in through your nose that then mixes with the mucous membrane that covers your olfactory epithelium.

With smell, one can objectively perceive the characteristics of many substances. All living creatures secrete odors via metabolic processes, breathing, glandular secretions, and so on, and for each function, each individual has his or her own odors. Of course, our personal odors can periodically be of a different strength and composition than usual. But even if a human—say a perpetrator of a crime—is giving off a particularly weak scent, you can count on dogs to be able to smell it. Dogs can observe organic compounds in human sweat diluted a million-fold.[2]

Odorous and Odorless

We are more able to describe and measure the conditions necessary for visual or auditory perception than we are to describe odors. Light, for example, allows us to see things; it makes things visible. We can measure light using objective parameters: the wavelength of light determines its color (measured in nanometers); the strength of light can be measured in lux. Sound can also be measured: the frequency determines the tone (measured in Hertz); the amount can be measured in decibels. Odor, however, cannot easily be measured.

One definition: an odor is that which can be smelled. But does that mean what we can smell? Or what a butterfly can smell? Or what a dog can smell? What do we mean when we say, for example, that something is "odorless"? Usually, we mean that the thing is something humans cannot smell. But it is a well-known fact that different people have different levels of sensitivity to odors. Therefore, we must be careful when using the words "odor" and "odorless."

It is, however, relatively easy to prove that something has an odor. If a person can smell it, or if you can train an animal to react to it, then it has an odor. But it is much more difficult to prove that something has no odor at all. Maybe a person with a very sensitive nose could smell the odor, or maybe the animal you trained to detect the odor was not trained correctly.

And there is another problem when it comes to measuring odors. One study on people used electroencephalograms (EEG) to establish characteristic brain-wave patterns that result when people smell an odor. During the study, researchers found that sometimes a person's brain reacts in the characteristic way to an odor, but the person may say he has not smelled anything.[3] So, what is an odor? That which you physically respond to (as in the case of the EEG measurement), or that which you are conscious of having smelled? At this time, there appears to be no correct answer to this question.

Odor is that which can be smelled. But does that mean what humans can smell or what a butterfly can smell? Perhaps it means what a dog can smell.

SOME CHARACTERISTICS OF ODOR

A few general characteristics of odor molecules—keeping in mind that all material consists of molecules—are:

- Odor molecules are relatively small: they must be light enough to float in the air. The molecular weight of an odor molecule is 300, maximum.
- Odor molecules are weakly polar: they have no strong magnetic parts.
- Odor molecules do not dissolve well in water. So if you try to remove an odor from an object, boiling that object in water will not be enough. To deodorize something, you must use water in combination with (non-perfumed) soap or another fat-dissolving product.
- Odor molecules dissolve in fats. The perfume industry understands this well. In the past, odorous plants (like lavender) were laid between fabric sheets that were soaked with an "odorless" fat and then left to sit for several days. The perfumer (sometimes called a Nose because of his or her fine sense of smell) would later dissolve the lavender-infused fat

PHEROMONES

Scent strongly influences sexual behavior. Salmon use their sense of smell to navigate inland during their reproductive period. Butterflies find each other over large distances by smell. And a sow likes a boar when he is producing a certain odor. Odorants that influence sexual behavior are called pheromones, water-soluble chemicals released and sensed by individuals of the same species and that elicit social and reproductive behaviors or physiologic changes; they are perceived primarily by the vomeronasal organ (a peripheral sensory organ that in most amphibians, mammals, and reptiles is located at the base of the nasal septum or in the roof of the mouth). Examples of pheromones include androstenediol, produced in the armpits of men, and the muskrat's musk.

Of course, the perfume industry has taken advantage of everything we know about pheromones. A lot of perfumes contain a little musk and even a little bit of the odor of excrements, which might seem odd. However, neither humans (especially children) nor dogs have an aversion to their own excrement. Consider that adults often sit on the toilet (reading) longer than really is necessary.

Women's menstrual cycles can also be influenced by odors. When women live together, they eventually menstruate synchronically. That this is a matter of odor was demonstrated during an experiment in which women who were not living together were supplied with each other's body odors. After a while, the menstrual periods were synchronized.[4]

in alcohol, thereby releasing the odor into a liquid that could then be used to make perfume.

Humans Odors

In general, all mammals produce several different odors. Expired air, urine, feces, exocrine glandular secretions, and emissions from body openings (mouth, nose, ears, anus, and the urogenital area) all contain odorous substances. Since the subject of this book concerns the individuality of human odor traces left on objects or soil at crime scenes, we will focus here on the odor of human skin. In general, the

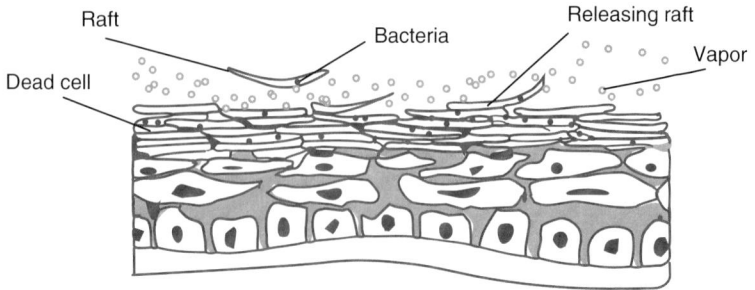

Dead cells, or rafts, flake off from the outside skin layer, carrying bacteria and an accompanying scent.

differences between individual skin odors are thought to be the sum of genetic differences, bacterial action, diet, and glandular secretions.

The skin itself is a continuous source of rafts, or dead cells that flake off from the skin surface. Rafts are left on the objects a person touches. If sufficient material is left behind, we can use modern DNA technology to analyze mitochondrial DNA sequences and thus identify whom the material came from. Rafts also flake off into the air and are carried away on air currents; we describe the new and unproven theory of "man trailing" related to these rafts in our books *K9 Fraud!* and *K9 Professional Tracking* (both published by Brush Education Inc.).

There are three kinds of glands that secrete directly onto the skin or into canals that lead to the skin surface, and some of these secretions are odorous. Such secretions left on a glass slide during fingerprinting remain discernable to dogs for some weeks, even if they haven't been preserved. Let's take a closer look at human skin and its glands.

HUMAN SKIN

The skin is the shield that separates the individual from the outside world. This organ protects the human body against influences from the environment and consists of several parts. The upper, or outside, layer is called the epidermis and the second layer is the

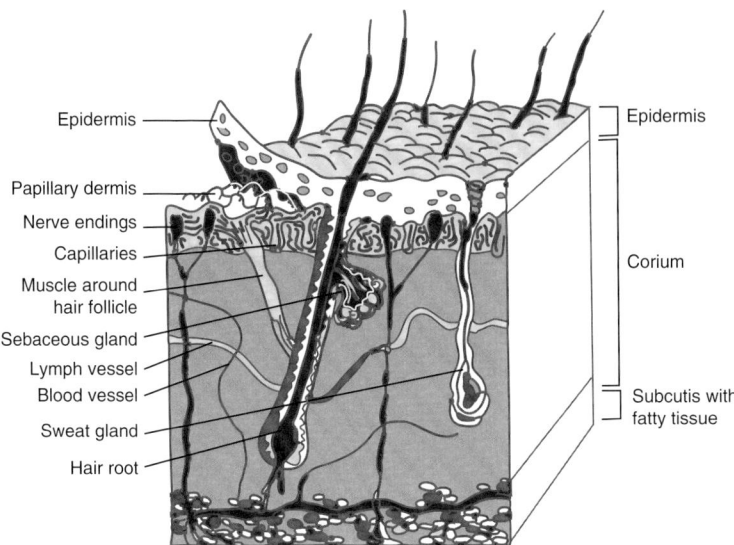

A schematic representation of human skin, showing the different layers, hair follicles, and sweat and sebaceous glands.

corium (or dermis), and these two layers form the skin. The subcutis is beneath the two upper layers, and under that lies the adipose tissue: both of these parts have important functions related to heat insulation and energy storage, and they both act as a physical buffer against bumps. In the skin we also find sebaceous glands, sweat glands, hair follicles (except for on the lips, palms, and soles of the feet), and the matrices from which finger and toenails form.

EPIDERMIS

The epidermis consists of two types of cells: melanocytes (pigment) and keratinocytes. In the basal layers of the skin (i.e., the stratum germinativum), columnar epithelial cells are found. These cells divide and move outward, passing through several cell layers to the skin's surface, the stratum corneum. During this process, these columnar epithelial cells first grow then form keratohyalin, and finally die. It is thought that lipids in the stratum corneum form the physical skin barrier that prevents bacteria from entering the body through the skin. (Lipids are free fatty acids, cholesterol, and ceramides.) In the stratum corneum, the columnar epithelial cells gradually flatten, shrink, and begin to lie loosely against each other. They then become keratinocytes (rafts), which peel off at a rate of 0.02 to 0.04 ounces (0.5–1 g) per day. Rafts are normally invisible, except for dandruff, which is released from the scalp, and the dead cells that are a consequence of certain skin diseases, such as psoriasis.

The epidermis varies in thickness, but it is normally only some tenths of a millimeter thick, no thicker than a thin membrane. On places where the skin is callused, like the palms of the hands and the soles of the feet, the epidermis is much thicker. Because new epidermal cells are constantly generated and old ones continually flaking off, the epidermis renews about once a month.

CORIUM

The corium is a one- to two-sixteenths of an inch (1 to 3 mm) thick layer of wavy, bulgy tissue that connects the papillary dermis to the epidermis. The bulges in the corium help connect these two layers of skin. The corium is filled with many little blood vessels (capillaries) that both convey nutrients and oxygen to the epidermis and carry waste away.

Farther down in the corium is the reticular dermis, which forms the bulk of the corium. This part contains a network of bigger blood and lymph vessels, which also supply nutrients to and take waste away from the sebaceous and sweat glands, and the muscles in hair follicles. The blood vessels in the skin are not only responsible for nourishing, oxygenating, and managing waste, but they also regulate body temperature. The reticular dermis is characterized by dense collagenous and elastic connective tissue. In the corium there are also a large number of nerve endings, which control the senses of touch, pain, and temperature.

SKIN GLANDS

There are three different kinds of glands in human skin that secrete substances onto the skin's surface and therefore contribute to skin odor. Two of these are typically called "sweat glands"—eccrine and apocrine glands—and the third are sebaceous glands.

HUMAN ODOR ON OBJECTS

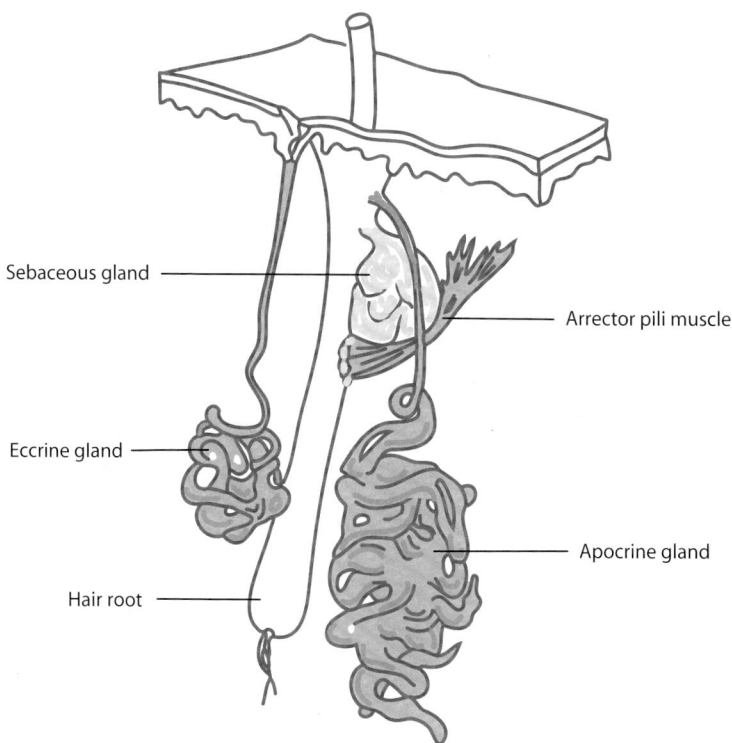

A schematic view of the three important glands near the hair root in the skin. The arrector pili muscle attaches to the hair follicle; when contracted, this muscle causes the hair to stand on end.

ECCRINE GLANDS

Two to four million eccrine glands exist all over the human body, and they produce a clear solution. More than 98 per cent of this solution consists of water, in which numerous organic and inorganic components are dissolved. Eccrine "sweat" plays a major role in the thermoregulation of the body. Because of body warmth and air currents around the body, sweat evaporates immediately after it secretes through skin pores onto the skin's surface. When the body sweats a lot, clothes that touch the skin absorb the sweat and its odor. During periods of high emotion or nervous tension, the eccrine glands that are in the forehead, the palms of the hands, and the soles of the feet secrete a large amount of sweat. In normal individuals, the eccrine glands can secrete as much as four to eight pints (2–4 L) per hour.

APOCRINE GLANDS

The apocrine glands are found in specific places on the human body, especially in the armpits and the genital area. They produce a cloudy, viscous solution containing large amounts of cholesterol. Bacteria on the skin break down apocrine sweat into odorous molecules, in particular steroids, which are thought to be biologically interesting signals, or pheromones.

According to A.I. Spielman and his associates, apocrine glands in the armpits are the source of human primer-type pheromones, the volatile odors that attract the attention of the opposite sex. Spielman and associates found that the chemistry of the odors of human apocrine gland secretions and that of non-human mammalian signaling odors is similar.[5] The axillary organ—the bundle of apocrine glands in the armpits—is not equally present in all humans and may even be missing in some. The size of an individual's axillary organ is connected to genetic background. These glands in the armpits are the major source of body odor as perceived by other people.

SEBACEOUS GLANDS

Sebaceous glands occur all over the body except on the palms of the hands and the soles of the feet. They are located beside hair follicles and discharge secretions into those structures. The sebum they produce seals hair shafts, thereby preventing the penetration of bacteria and the loss of water. Sebum consists of all sorts of fatty substances that keep the skin pliable and hydrated. When we move our bodies, sebum spreads over the surface of our skin, and so also comes to protect the palms of our hands and soles of our feet.

On average, there are about 100 sebaceous glands per half-inch squared (1 cm^2). The number of these glands increases to almost one thousand per half-inch squared on the middle of our chests

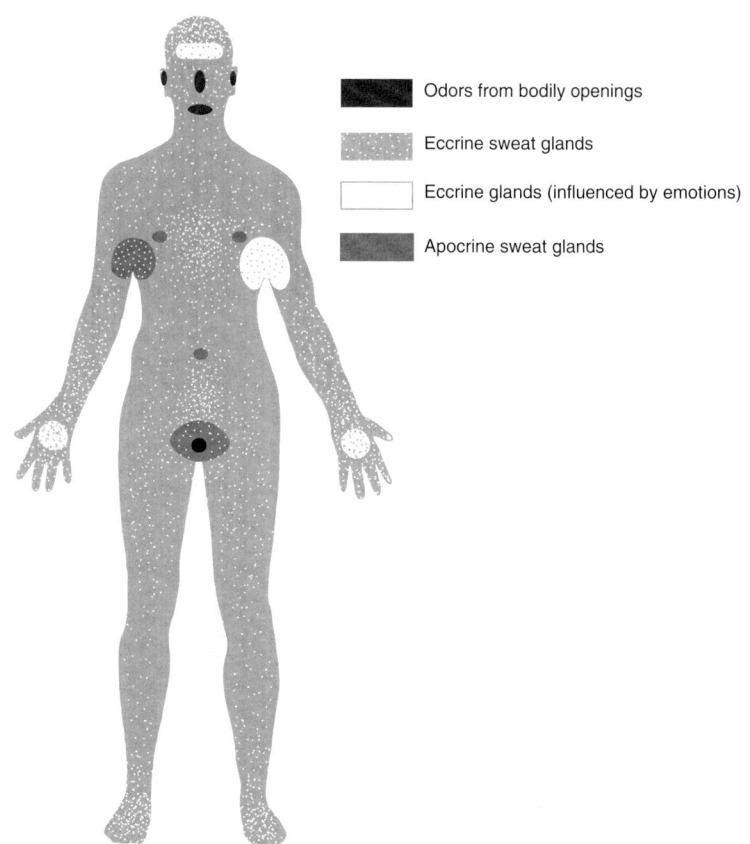

Distribution of the different sweat glands over the human body.

and on our backs, faces, and scalps. Those who produce a lot of sebum often have to manage greasy hair.

The sebaceous glands are a type of holocrine gland, which means they secrete whole cells that have broken down to transport them from the body. Sebaceous glands secrete sebum by partially breaking down and releasing a gland cell into a pore in the skin. In the pores, the sebum and the remains of the cell are further broken down by lypolisis, a process driven by enzymes derived from the epidermis and bacteria. It takes eight to 10 days from formation of the cell until it has broken down and its products (mainly triglycerides and free fatty acids) can be found on the skin. These fatty acid products are thought to form the olfactory signature of an individual. Support for this comes from examining non-human mammals' scent-marking glands; glands known to provide information about the identity of an individual produce sebaceous lipids.

Rates of sebum excretion, amounts of certain fatty acids, the ratio of wax esters to cholesterol, and cholesterol esters change with age.

LIFE ON THE SKIN

Both the products of the apocrine and sebaceous glands are broken down into odorous compounds by bacteria in skin pores and on the skin. Let's take a close look at these bacteria.

The skin's microflora includes such bacteria as micrococcadeae, staphylococci, corynebacterium acnes, pityrosporum ovale, pityrosporum acnes, pityrosporum granulosum, and propionibacteria. Several studies, such as one conducted by E.A. Eady and associates in 1994, have shown that treatment of the skin with topical antibiotics decreases bacterial populations and thus contributes to a loss of fatty acids.[6] However, some bacteria remain unaffected by antibiotics, probably because they are present in the hair follicles and out of reach.

Different bacterial populations are found in different body areas, and these populations remain quite stable over time.[7] The consequence of these regional population differences is that different areas of one individual body have different odors.

The regions with the largest numbers of bacteria are the face, the neck, the armpits and the groin, as well as the soles of the feet and between the toes. Bear in mind, however, that the differences in bacterial population between people are quite large.

With increasing age, human skin's microflora undergoes qualitative changes, probably because of hormonal changes and changes in sebum production. As children grow up, streptococci populations disappear and coryneform bacteria populations increase. The latter type of bacteria is mainly responsible for odor production.

Anaerobic propionibacteria are more numerous in juveniles and young adults than any other age group. Only coryneform bacteria are able to produce axillary odor through the decomposition of apocrine sweat.

LIPIDS

It seems that the lipids on human skin are the substances most likely to cause each person to have a unique scent, so they merit some attention. For the most part, lipids are the products of sebum, produced by sebaceous glands. The small number of lipids on the skin that are not part of sebum come from the epidermis and from contamination (for example, through shaking hands), which can be minimized by frequent washing.

As mentioned above, sebaceous glands are holocrine glands, in fact, the only holocrine glands that exist in the human body. Some of the lipids in sebum are cell lipids (or epidermal lipids) and others are specialized lipids synthesized by the cell (endogeneous lipids). This synthesized part is thought to have the most influence on the composition of the secreted sebum. Approximately 37 per cent of the fatty acids found on the skin are "biologically valuable"; the remaining 63 per cent consists of more than 200 different kinds of free fatty acids ranging from very small to very large (C7 to C30[8]). Some of these are very unusual; for example, sebaleic acid seems to be a surface lipid that is unique to human skin.

The chemical content of skin lipids changes with age. In 2001 R.S. Ramotowski summarized these changes, which include rates of sebum secretion and the amounts of certain fatty acids. Ramotowski also concluded that some components of sebum do not change significantly as the body ages.[9] Young children do not produce much sebum, and their lipid composition is dominated by cholesterol and cholesterol esters, which are primarily of epidermal origin. As hormonal stimulation increases in puberty, more sebum is produced. Peak production happens when a person reaches his or her mid-thirties. Females have lower sebum secretion levels than males, and people with acne have higher secretion levels than people without acne. The stimulation of the sebaceous glands results in a change in lipid composition on the skin: more endogeneously (or internally) produced lipids are found, and the epidermal lipids remain relatively constant. Overall, the secretion levels and sebum composition remain constant from puberty until much later in life (males over 70, females over 50). The principle reason behind this decline is diminished hormonal stimulation.

There are large individual differences between adults in terms of lipid composition and relative amounts of lipid groups. The inter-individual differences in amounts of free fatty acids, cholesterol, and ceramides in the stratum corneum, for example, can be more than 100 per cent. A study using just two donors showed that certain fatty acids seem to vary in concentration within a seven-week timespan,[10] but a later study using 10 subjects concluded that the composition of the fatty acids appeared to remain stable over a two-month period.[11] Different studies have concluded that it seems unlikely that fluctuations occur as a result of diet or metabolism.[12]

Researchers who compared the lipid composition of identical twins and unrelated people found evidence for genetic control of lipid composition.[13] This work on lipids and genes relates to other research being conducted on genetic control of body odors.

Human Skin and Odor

A large body of work about the genetic control of urine odors has shown the significant role of the major histocompatability complex (MHC).[14] The MHC is a group of genes connected to the immune system. In humans it is called Human Leucocyte Antigen (HLA) and the genes are located on chromosome 7. Nowadays, theories about the genetic control of odors include the interactions between immune system antigens and bacteria: the antigens (or their breakdown products) could influence the commensal bacterial flora and thus individual body odor. This area of study could be important for forensic scientists working with odors. As

Boyse states, "Odor profiles governed by HLA could be more distinctive than fingerprints with respect to genetic identity, because the genetic component of fingerprints is uncertain."[15]

As we now know, regional differences in microflora on the skin mean that different body parts have their own particular odors. To humans, armpit odor smells totally different from genital odor, which in turn smells different from the soles of the feet. In fact, Löhner found that for humans, the similarity of scent between the same regions of different people seems to be greater than that of different regions of the same person.[16]

This does not mean that an individual does not have a unique odor, however; in fact, Löhner found that for dogs, the similarity in the smell of different body areas of the same person was greater than the similarity of odors between the same areas belonging to different people.

There is also some evidence that the dog's ability to focus on a human being's one, overarching odor is the result of training: dogs trained to detect the hand odor of their handlers had difficulty when asked to choose between the hand odor of a stranger and a non-hand odor (for example, odor from the crook of the elbow) of their handler, and dogs trained to match objects scented in pockets to the hand odor of the individual who had handled the objects performed better in trials than dogs that had to match the hand odor of an individual to that same person's odor coming from the crook of the elbow.

The importance of genetics to human odor is also evident in the results of behavioral studies where the difference between the odors of identical twins, siblings, or other genetically related people is smaller than differences between odors of non-related people. The stability of this "typical" odor is also clear from these studies: siblings recognize each other's odor on T-shirts after not having seen each other for more than two years.[17]

Recent behavioral studies have begun to examine the effect of variations in immune system genes (MHC or HLA genes).

Women seem to prefer the odors produced by men who have distinctly different HLA genes than they have. This can be explained in terms of sexual selection: by mating with such a genetically different person, offspring will have a broader spectrum of immune system genes and thus be healthier. In another study, it was found that women were able to identify people who had immune system genes similar to those of their fathers.[18]

Now that we understand that unique human odor is controlled by our genes, we can begin to discuss the stability and sources of variation of an individual's odor, the stability of individual odors left on objects, and the mixing of odors that occurs when different people touch the same object.

Stability of Human Odor

It seems unlikely that one could easily alter one's own unique odor: if a person's genetic makeup influences the microflora responsible for the composition of fatty acids on the skin, the only way to change one's scent would be to purposely change one's bacterial microflora. Products that minimize axillary odor by modifying microflora to produce less odor are, of course, ongoing sources of income for the pharmaceutical and cosmetics industries, and they illustrate the difficulty of masking or minimizing such odor. Research has found that applying antibiotics to the skin diminishes bacterial populations, but these are usually only applied locally, so the rest of the body continues to generate odors.

Although a person's diet seems to have an effect on his or her odor, lipids derived from diet are in the minority in the skin lipids, and the long turnover time of the sebaceous cells (between eight and 10 days) prevents rapid changes as a result of intake.

Washing also minimizes the amount of lipids on the skin, and therefore odor, but the effect is only short-term because lipids are replenished quickly. Human odor is pervasive and, as we've noted, stable. Recall the study that proved siblings can recognize each other's recent odor even after a 30-month separation. For forensic purposes, the stability over time of an odor left on an object is vitally important.

Odor on Objects

The odor traces left on objects connected to a crime must be stable to be of any use to forensic experts, since the period between when the perpetrator deposited the odor and when comparisons are made between that odor and that of a suspect can be considerable, from weeks to years. In general, scent marks that linger for a long time are produced by sebaceous glands, but even these odors have a best-before date, and environmental conditions can affect how long an odor remains stable on an object.

Direct sunlight, in particular, breaks down many organic substances, and some microorganisms (bacteria and fungi) feed on organic components such as those in odors. In a study done by the Pacific Northwest National Laboratory, researchers examined the chemical changes in latent fingerprint deposits over a 30-day period. They found that saturated fatty compounds remain relatively stable. However, unsaturated lipids (such as squalene and some of the fatty acids) diminished substantially within the 30-day period, especially during the first week. With time, more saturated, low-molecular acids appeared, originating from the breaking down of the unsaturated lipids. In aged samples, the saturated components dominated.[19]

The essential question for forensic purposes: how long can human odor on an object retain its unique identity for a dog? The fingerprint study noted above has been confirmed by instructors who have taught dogs to make scent identification matches using aged objects. Objects aged up to a week have to be trained step by step and seem to be relatively difficult for dogs. However, as soon as a dog is trained to deal with week-old scents on objects, he can easily manage scent matches with objects holding much older scents. A study conducted with Dutch scent-identification dogs and objects holding aged scents showed that the dogs' success rates

The odor traces left on objects at a crime scene or connected to a crime must be stable for investigators to use them. After all, the period of time between the perpetrator depositing the odor and the process wherein the odor is compared to that of a suspect can be considerable, from weeks to years.

dropped significantly from when they were working with freshly scented (zero days) to two-week-old scented objects. The success rates were stable, however, with objects that were holding scents from two weeks to six months.[20] This, too, aligns with the fingerprint study.

Mixing of Odors

Another question that is both interesting and important to forensic work with odors: what happens when odors of different individuals are superimposed on each other, as could happen when there are several perpetrators of a crime or when the object used in a crime is stolen? Chemically, these odors would mix into a new compound that contains fatty acids from all individuals involved. Behavioral experiments with golden hamsters and meadow voles indicate that when two scent marks are superimposed on each other, only the top odor is perceived or considered important. How the animals are able to do this is not yet fully discovered, but the term "olfactory occlusion" has been used to describe the phenomenon.[21]

Anecdotal evidence from dog handlers indicates that dogs are capable of recognizing each of the two mixed odors, but this ability declines as the scents on the object age. This "scent age" is the period between when the object is handled and when the dog and his handler work with the object.

In 1955 H. Kalmus noted that dogs were able to recognize superimposed odors: one dog had been trained to pick out a handkerchief scented a few minutes in one person's armpit among several other, similarly scented handkerchiefs. This dog was also able to pick out this person's handkerchief if the odor had been overlaid by the scent from another person's armpit, or by an artificial odor.[22]

Löhner observed the same phenomenon in a scent-matching test using human scents on pieces of wood. Even if the piece of wood was kept in hand for only one or two seconds, or if it was touched with a fingertip for two minutes, the dog in the study succeeded in matching it to the odor's owner. "Even if the odor of another person clings to the same piece of wood, the dog could make the correct choice."[23]

In 2000, Polish researcher M. Rogowski did more work related to the dog's ability to identify layered scents. Person A was given the worn trousers of person B to wear, after which he had to sit down in a car belonging to person C. After this, a scent sample was taken from the car seat. Dogs were able to distinguish the odors of all three persons related to the scent sample.[24] In conclusion, we can say that dogs, like other animals, are capable of discerning the odors of different individuals on an object, which means that we can use dogs to help us in scent-identification line-ups or in other procedures related to scent.

3

Human Odor on a Track

We may accept that the odors from bodily openings (mouth, nose, ears, anus, and the urogenital area) may not influence the odor complex on a human's "track" (the physical and scented trail left behind by a person moving through the world). These odors, however, can be helpful to search-and-rescue dogs as they perform their duties. In particular, the odors of breath and sometimes urine (excreted during panic or excitement) can be important odor sources for dogs.

Some trainers believe that the individual odor of the tracklayer plays no particular role in a dog's ability to track that person. According to them, other factors determine the viability of a track: the odor of the shoes worn when making the track and differences in the shoe size and weight of tracklayers, who sink more or less into the soil, damage plants, and in doing so cause stronger or weaker odors to be emitted from the soil and damaged foliage. In their opinion, the odor of the tracklayer exists in such a small quantity on the track that, even when it is present, it disappears beneath the other track odors.

Others believe the individual human odors on a track are what dogs should search for when tracking. These people believe that a well-trained dog can only stay on the track—even over difficult

Can dogs perceive human odor on a track?

surfaces, such as a paved road, and not be diverted by cross-tracks made around the same time as the track they are following—when searching for a particular human odor.

What Is Perceptible for the Dog?

So, can dogs perceive the human odor component of a track or not? Dr. W. Neuhaus set out to answer this question when he conducted a study in which he calculated human sweat production and sweat odors. These he compared with the dog's very low threshold values for odors, which he had already determined in earlier experiments. He concluded that the amount of human odor present on a normal track, even hours after the track has been laid, is enough to be perceptible to a dog.[1]

Neuhaus's conclusion was based on the threshold values for separate, clearly discernable odor substances. But human odor is a mixture of odors. As a follow up, therefore, Neuhaus investigated the base amount of multiple odor substances required to prickle olfactory receptors, and he found lower threshold values for such mixtures than for each of the mixture's different odor substances offered separately. His earlier conclusion that dogs could perceive human odor in the track was therefore strengthened.[2]

COMPETING ODORS

Neuhaus found that even if an odor is accompanied by another, stronger odor, dogs can observe small deviations in the odor mix that allow them to differentiate between the dominant odor and the underlying one. This explains the observation that a dog can recognize the odor of a human and an object touched by that human, even when the object has a stronger odor than that of the human, or has another strong odor on it.

When a dog is working out the scent on a track, he may encounter such competing odors, as when the track shifts from a meadow to a wood. Even when the other odor components of the track are about a thousand times stronger than the human odor, it is still possible for the dog to recognize the human odor.

SWEATY FEET

In his book, *Scent and the Scenting Dog*, W.G. Syrotuck provides the table on page 37 with the average number of eccrine sweat glands per square centimetre on different parts of the human body.

The sebum and sweat secretions from the skin on human feet and soles figure dominantly in research about tracking dogs. As this table shows, the soles of the human feet, in particular, are equipped with a large number of eccrine sweat glands, which produce sweat that includes dissolved volatile fatty acids. Besides that, the many sebaceous glands on the sides and tops of the feet,

Eccrine Sweat Glands in Humans

Part of the Body	Average Number (per cm^2)
Sole of the foot	600
Forehead	360
Top of the foot	250
Forearm	225
Trunk	175
Upper arm	150
Leg	130[3]

and the influence of bacteria on the sebum they secrete, contribute heavily to the presence of even more fatty acids.

In 1990 Dr. F. Kanda compared the fatty acids from the socks and feet of people with strong foot odor to those of people with weak foot odor. People with strong foot odor were found to produce larger amounts of fatty acids than those with weak or negligible foot odor. One of the fatty acids, isovalerianic acid, was present in all people with perceptible foot odor but was not detected in those without.[4]

The soles of the feet transfer these fatty acids onto any surface they touch. Even if a person is wearing socks or shoes and there is no direct contact between a surface and bare feet, the fatty acids are unhindered and still penetrate through whatever is between them and the contact surface.

Because of constant evaporation of the watery parts of sweat through the pores, and the fact that the material of socks and shoes easily absorbs fluids, intensely smelly substances accumulate. All footwear becomes fully drenched by the odors produced by the fatty acids.

Our feet sweat all the time (often without us noticing), and, through the porous soles of the shoes (and along their edges), a constant stream of moisture and odor-producing substances come out. When the soles touch the ground, the moisture and odors are

When shoes wear out, the worn areas, holes, and tears provide places where foot odor can directly emerge, thereby increasing the human odor of a track.

precipitated (the odor substances separated out from the moisture) and pressed together. With every step, even those that take only a fraction of a second, a direct diffusion of volatile fatty acids comes through the soles and is left on the ground.

As we walk, we move our feet in our shoes, which increases the diffusion of gaseous foot sweat through the soles of our shoes. Foot odor is not contained by our shoes; when we walk, applying pressure to the ground, we push the odor out through the pores and seams of our shoes.

Worn-out shoes are especially good at spilling foot odor, increasing the odor of our footprints. But there is more. The sweat accumulated in footwear and our soles can be drawn from the material of the shoes (leather, rubber, fabric, and so on) by fluid. Part of fatty acids is readily soluble in water. If our shoes come into contact with moist or even wet ground, that water dissolves some of the sweat stored in the shoes, adding its odors to our footprints. Thus, with every step we take on wet ground, the sweat stored in our shoes spreads: it is pressed out by the motion and pressure of walking and absorbed in our footprints, and thus the track. On a hard, dry surface, of course, less odor transfer takes place. We can observe this in practice. A dog can follow a track on moist ground more easily than one on dry soil.

FOOT AND SHOE

The front part of the foot normally gives off more odor than any other part of the foot because many sweat glands are located there, and the sebum between the toes is more quickly attacked by bacteria (because it is warm there). The heel, made of thicker skin and fewer sweat glands, contributes less to the odor we leave behind when we walk. The front part of our feet also has a thinner sole and wears quicker than the heel, so odorous substances emerge easily from the pores, the humidity from the sweat produced at the front of the foot helping to quickly spread the odors.

The front part of the foot sweats a lot more than the back or middle, not only because of all the extra sweat glands but also because it is always flexing when we walk or run; body parts that move sweat more than those that don't move. As well, while we walk, the front part of the foot rubs against the sole of the shoe more than the back part does—and the toes rub against each other—and so sweat and sebum production and release is higher here than in the other parts of the foot. In short, the front part of our feet and shoes is smellier than the middle or back parts, and so this part of the foot leaves the most scent on a track. Remember, too, that as we walk, the front parts of our feet stay the longest on the ground. As we shift forward in our stride, we press the whole weight of our bodies on the balls of our feet, although only for a fraction of a second, grinding that part of our shoes into the ground.

As we contemplated passage of odors from human feet onto a track, we became interested in determining how much odor the sides and tops of shoes allow through. To answer this question, we poured water into an old waterproofed leather climbing boot, up to the place where the shaft begins. After half a minute, the leather sides of the boot were saturated and the outside was moist. When Ruud put the boot on, beads of water formed on the

When tracking, we improve our ability to read a track by employing the sensory perception of our dogs.

outside surface of the boot, coming through the invisible pores in the leather, in particular in those places where the leather was creased by wear. Every time Ruud took a step forward in the boot and the material flexed, the leather was pressed together so that the outside was moistened. After performing this little experiment, it was clear to us how powerfully foot odor (which is mostly gaseous and therefore emerges much easier from a shoe than the water in our experiment) is conveyed from inside a shoe to outside it.

Odor and Natural Influences

As you can see, every step you take transfers your unique human odor onto your track; the surface of each of your footprints is covered with fatty acids from the eccrine sweat and sebum affected by bacteria. Just like any other substance lying on Earth's surface, however, fatty acids are subject to dissipation or change. Odor can be affected by natural factors such as instability of the fatty acids, wind, temperature, sunlight, soil, and water.

Left in a pristine environment, fatty acids won't change or disappear very easily. If, for example, sweat odor in clothes or articles is preserved in the right way (in a tightly closed, glass jar) then removed and presented to a dog, he will be able to smell it even if the article has been in the jar for a very long time.

Of course, we cannot preserve a track in this fashion. Air movement stimulates the evaporation of fatty acids on a track. Consider also that a windblown track is spread out over a large area. If the wind deposits sand or other material onto the track, tracking can become more difficult, depending on the covering and age of the track.

We know that the temperature variations and limits in nature are not great enough to affect fatty acids. The influence of direct sunlight on a track, however, is less known. From experiments, we know that odors preserved in glass jars do not change even after days of intensive solar rays. On the track, however, the heat of the sun increases evaporation. So, during warm and dry weather, the odor on a track will go away sooner than on cooler, more humid days.

Track surfaces also influence the staying power of odors. Take the example of wood. On the one hand, wood that is dry and not covered with paint or varnish, such as on bridges or planks that span ditches, absorbs sweat with its fatty acids and holds it, probably without changing the scent. Fresh wood, on the other hand, contains all sorts of active chemical substances, such as etheric oils that, upon making contact with sweat, eventually change the fatty acids.

Untreated concrete, paving stones, and bricks, because of capillary repulsion, absorb fluids very easily. The pebbles and sand that make up these surfaces are chemically neutral to the fatty acids in sweat. Raw limestone and marble, however, just like all other carbon-based minerals, break down fatty acids.

Newly laid asphalt and asphalt-concrete roads contain chemical substances that have a disinfecting effect on fatty acids deposited on a track, influencing their chemical structure. The breakdown of fatty acids left on old asphalt roads, however, is slower than on new asphalt.

Newly laid asphalt and asphalt-concrete roads contain chemical substances that have a disinfecting effect on fatty acids deposited on a track, influencing their chemical structure. Old asphalt roads don't affect fatty acids as much.

When it is left behind on humus, the odor in sweat is lost because living microbes, acids (humus acids), and bases are all at work, constantly cleaning the environment, and they break down sweat just as they break down whatever else they come across. Ammonia in soil can also be a factor to consider, as it easily combines with fatty acids to form fatty acid salts—the resulting structural change makes the compounds less detectable.

The presence and amount of water on a track is crucial in tracking. Because some fatty acids are liquid at ambient temperature, they dissolve easily in water derived from atmospheric precipitation (dew, rain, snow) and soak into the soil on a track. If rain or snow falls on the track, odors are diluted, washed away, or covered up, making tracking difficult for the dog. However, if rain or snow falls before the track is laid, tracking is made easier. Moist ground favors the process of odor spreading as the odor is transferred from the feet and pressed into and through footwear.

On soft or snowy ground, the pressure of a person's body weight can cause wells or depressions in the ground surface, creating an odor-filled reservoir from which odors do not readily escape. Dogs can easily work out tracks with these odor-filled dips.

WATER, TEMPERATURE, AND EVAPORATION OF FATTY ACIDS ON A TRACK

We haven't yet fully explored the influence of water on a track. A dog can work out a track laid on moistened terrain better than one laid on the warm surface of a dry, sandy road. He can also work out an older track better on a humid or dewy morning or evening than on a warm afternoon. Temperature and humidity (water) play important roles in the viability of a track relative to fatty acids in sweat.

Fatty acids—like water and alcohol—evaporate faster when the air temperature is higher. If an air current (wind) is blowing over fatty acids, evaporation happens more readily and quickly than if the temperature is the same and there is no wind. When evaporating, fatty acid molecules change into a gaseous state without changing chemically. Like other liquids that change to gases, gaseous fatty acids expand in the air and spread out to occupy the available space. The higher the temperature is, the more they spread out, gradually becoming more and more difficult for the olfactory system to perceive.

If fatty acid evaporation takes place in a small, closed room, the fatty acids saturate the air in the room with odor molecules. When saturation occurs, evaporation stops. If evaporation takes place outside during calm weather, the air layer directly above the surface of the fatty acids is the first to become saturated. Only then, by slow diffusion, will the odor vapor rise to the layer of air above. If the temperature rises, the diffusion process is faster and the air around the place where the fatty acids were deposited will more quickly become saturated by the diffused gases that result from evaporation.

A dog can work out a track laid on moistened terrain better than one laid on the warm surface of a dry, sandy road.

So, given what we now know, the following applies to fatty acids that are left behind in a footprint:

1. The higher the temperature, the faster the fatty acids on a track evaporate and the more odor vapor the air absorbs (to the point of saturation). In this manner, the gas molecules that are the product of fatty acid evaporation spread through the local air. In this scenario, because it is diluted in the air, the odor in the fatty acid gases are more difficult to perceive than if they were relegated to existing in the layer of air directly above the place where the fatty acids were deposited.

2. When the weather is calm, evaporation of fatty acids on a track is hindered to a point because the air immediately above them quickly becomes saturated, and so diffusion to the layer of air above that layer is slow going. From this it can be deduced that warmth and air currents (wind) can effectively erase the "smellable" track relatively quickly. On a windy and warm day, odor substances do not hang in the layer of air directly above the track, but they rise with

ease through layers of air and become so diluted that they escape our perception, or that of our dogs.

Cool temperatures and humid air are the best conditions to preserve an odor track. As the temperature rises, however, humid air will more quickly absorb odor substances than dry air.

One might say that a track is best preserved in cool and humid weather, but tracks exist in an ever-changing environment. The air has only to cool down a little (say, 1°C) and it may suddenly be unable to hold all of the water vapor it had previously been holding. In this case, some of that vapor will fall to the ground as dew. Fear not, dew does not damage the track! If the temperature, however, decreases by more than 1°C, rain or snow may fall and tracking becomes difficult.

A track retains its odor best when the temperature remains constant. Thus, the dog's tracking ability can be expected to be the most successful under the following conditions:

1. At the time of track-laying, the soil is moist.
2. Until tracking has begun, the air remains cold, calm, and (almost) saturated with water vapor.
3. The temperature of the air and ground stay the same from when the track was laid to when tracking is performed.

MOIST SOIL, DRY SOIL

We should examine one more consideration relative to tracks and their ability to hold odors. When the air is humid, the soil also absorbs water (dew). Dogs always track better on moist ground than on dry ground. To illustrate this fact, we worked out the following experiment. We dried a piece of filter paper that had been drenched with foot sweat (obtained by laying filter paper in a pair of shoes). When the paper was dry, it gave off almost no odor perceptible to us. But, when we used a plant mister to spray some water on the paper, we immediately perceived an intense sweat odor.

When the sweat-drenched paper dried, the fatty acids lying on its surface evaporated. The filter paper, swelled up with sweat, shrank as it dried and in doing so sealed off the odors that existed deeper in the paper, preventing them from evaporating. A certain amount of fatty acids, producing odor, was stored in small "rooms," if you will, in the paper.

When we misted the paper, these "rooms" were unlocked as the paper expanded to absorb the water. The stored odor substances (fatty acids dissolved in water) were then brought to the paper's surface by the liquid and become a solution of fatty acids spread over the whole surface of the paper. When the odorous solution spread out, the process of evaporation began again, and then we perceived the strong odor. A similar situation comes into play when frost preserves the scent of the track—only when thaw sets in is the scent released.

If the paper, however, is too-heavily moistened with water, the odor is less pungent, because the fatty acids are greatly diluted, and the fatty acids deep in the paper rise more slowly to the surface to evaporate.

Rubber, leather, and all the other materials used to make footwear—as well as shoe polishes or chemicals used for waterproofing—have their own specific odors, which together form the specific odor of the footwear.

When someone walks over dry soil, the ground absorbs the odor of his or her feet. Immediately after that, evaporation of the fatty acids that produce the odor begins. Odorants that have penetrated the soil more deeply do not evaporate as quickly as those lying on the dry surface of the ground.

If, overnight, the soil becomes moistened, however—by dew, let's say—what happened with our sweat-drenched and dried filter paper takes place on the track. Evaporation allows the dog's nose to perceive the odors that were heretofore "locked up" in the dry "rooms" in the soil. In addition, the moist air layer above the track slowly becomes saturated by odorous gases and, usually, in the morning and the evening, the air is calmer than it is during the day. Such a scenario is perfect for tracking. It must also be said that dogs track better in moist conditions because a moistened olfactory mucous membrane works better than a dry one.

THE BEST CIRCUMSTANCES

A track laid in dry conditions can best be tracked if a thin film of fluid (dew) is laid on it shortly before a dog is sent to work it out.

It is a well-known fact that a dog can work out an older track better on a humid or dewy morning or evening than on a warm afternoon.

This misting of water breathes new life into odorants lurking in what was dry soil. A slight warming of the ground and air also helps.

If the track is laid in moist or even wet weather, the best circumstances for the tracking dog arise when (in calm conditions and vapor-saturated air) the temperature rises slightly shortly before the dog starts tracking. The increase in temperature will spur on evaporation and send gaseous odors into the air just above the track.

Even if an odor is surrounded by a different odor, a dog can detect small deviations in the odor mix.

4

The Dog's Nose

Thanks to his ancestors, wolves, the dog possesses a highly developed olfactory system. Most predators find their prey by smell. They also recognize family and enemies by the tracks individual animals have left and the scent of their droppings and urine. Their olfactory systems give them the information they need to survive, picking up chemical messages from the outside world that are then conveyed to the brain as signals the brain understands. Once this process is complete, they can respond in the correct way to the stimulus. The following short description of the dog's olfactory system should provide you with a clear understanding of the dog's ability to perceive odors.

The External Nose

The dog's skull has a frontal and a nasal bone. The latter contains the olfactory system, the nose, in which there is a front part, the external nose, and an internal part. The external nose carries out important functions comparable to the functions of the external ear, which takes care of sound transmission to the brain.

The external nose picks up air turbulence and conducts odors to the internal nose by means of the cartilage and strong, muscled structure of the forenose. The forenose is the lightly moist, bald part

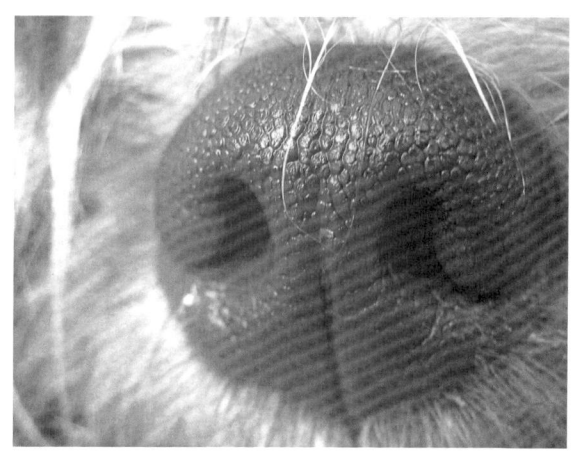

The surface of the forenose is unique for every dog. In fact, a dog's forenose print can be used to identify individual animals, just as we use fingerprints to identify specific humans.

of the upper lip of the dog, usually black (although it can be brown or gray depending, for instance, on the color of the dog's coat). The surface of the forenose is unique for every dog. In fact, a print of the forenose can be used for dog identification, just as fingerprints are used to identify humans. According to Dr. J. Bodingbauer, dogs with large forenoses are capable of greater scent achievements than dogs with small forenoses.[1]

In the forenose are situated both nostrils, which are the entrance to the internal nasal cavities. Sniffing causes the nostrils to widen and narrow; in this way, the dog controls the amount of air allowed in the nasal cavity. This means dogs can let less air in if they expect an odor to be uncommon or dangerous. The muscles in the external nose of adult dogs are well developed.

By sniffing, and turning his head and body, a dog can locate the source of an odor. A moistened mucous membrane—made thus by secretions from Bowman's glands (see description below)—in the nose also helps the dog to locate an odor source, much in the same way that a wet finger raised in the air allows us to determine wind direction.

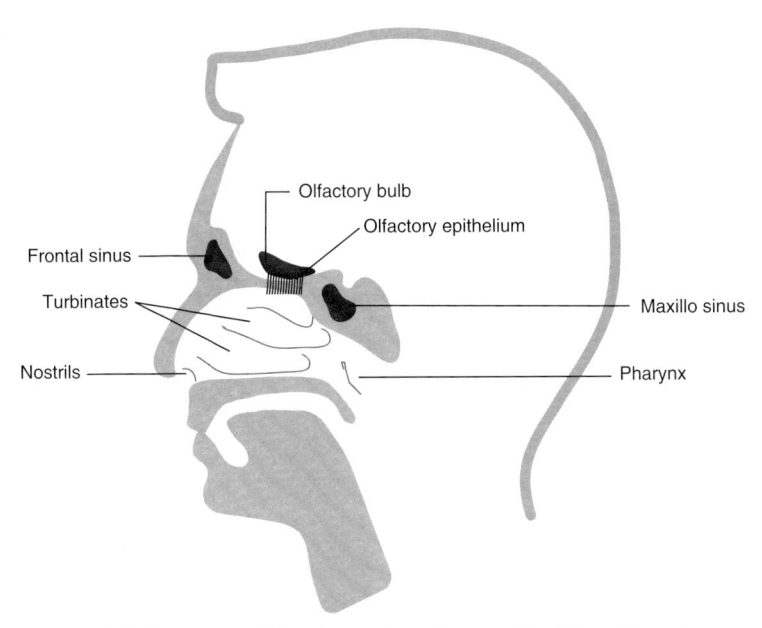

Anatomy of the human nose. When humans breathe normally, air flows through the lower and middle turbinates (also known as nasal conchae). Only by diffusion or sniffing does odor come through the upper turbinate and reach the olfactory epithelium.

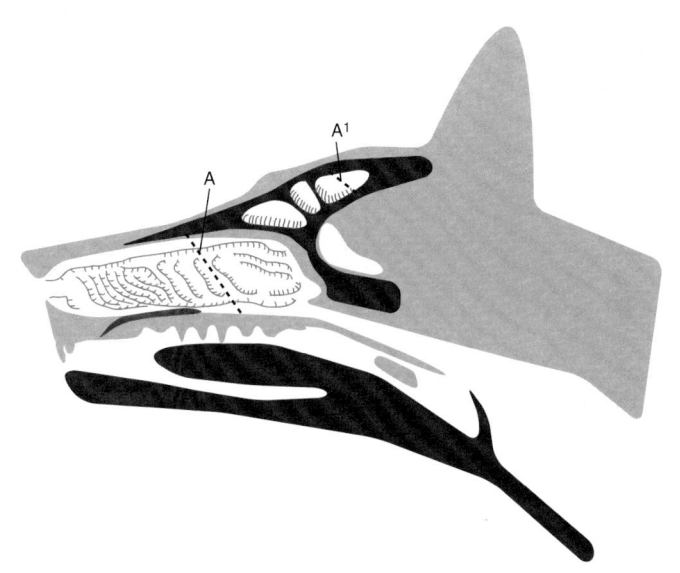

Size of the olfactory epithelium of the dog. A = front border and A^1 = rear border of the parts of the nasal cavity and the sinuses covered with olfactory epithelium.

The Internal Nose

In the internal nose, separated by the nasal septum, exist the left and right nasal cavities. The structure of the internal nose differs, depending on the species. Some animals are microsmatic (osmé = smell), or have poor odor perception (people, monkeys, chamois, and birds), while others, like dogs, are macrosmatic and have excellent olfactory function. In a microsmatic organism, only a small part of the nasal cavity is given to the olfactory epithelium (*regio olfactoria*), while the biggest part is used for normal breathing.

The nasal cavity of a macrosmatic, however, is a labyrinth of folds (nasal conchae or turbinates), which for the most part are covered with olfactory epithelium. Because of this labyrinth of turbinates, the surface of the internal nose is much larger in macrosmatic organisms than in microsmatics. The turbinates are situated from the side face of the nose to the septum, but they have no connection with the septum. Like the rest of the internal surface of the nose, the turbinates are covered with a mucous membrane that is richly supplied with blood and sensory neurons (olfactory cells).

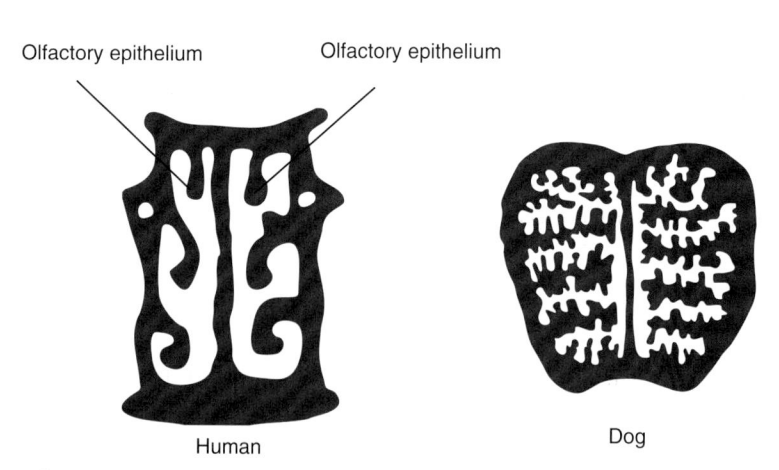

Left: A schematic representation of the transverse section of the human nose. The olfactory epithelium is only on the upper turbinates. Right: The same section of the dog's nose; notice the labyrinth of folds.

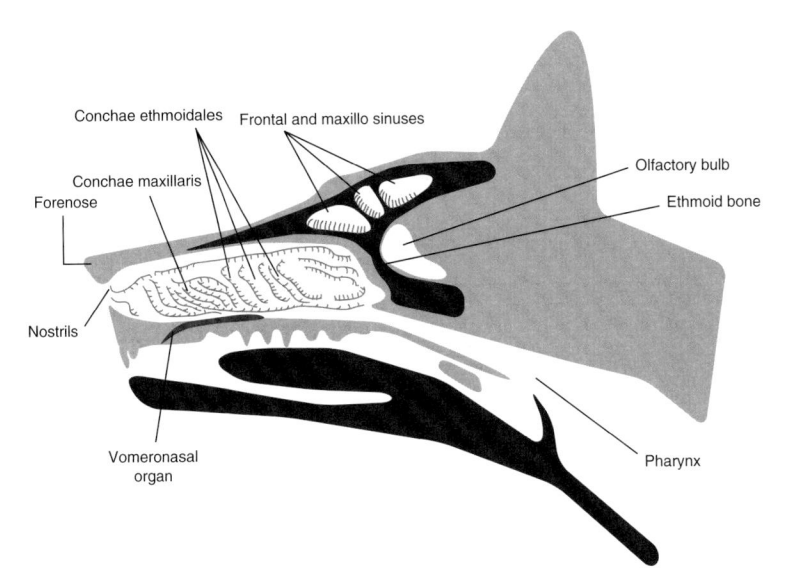

Anatomy of the dog's nose. With every in- and exhalation through the nose, the dog guides odors to the conchae (also known as turbinates) and the olfactory epithelium.

In front of the nasal cavity we find the conchae maxillaris, of which the mucous membrane, compared to the conchae ethmoidalis behind it, has fewer olfactory cells. The most important function of the turbinates of the conchae maxillaris is to warm and moisten incoming air. The mucous membrane of the conchae maxillaris contains many cells with vibrating hairs that help keep dirt out of the nasal cavity. Dirt that makes contact with the vibrating hairs is swept out and away by the vibrations.

Behind the conchae maxillaris we find the conchae ethmoidalis, which fills the rest of the nasal cavity. The mucous membrane on these turbinates contains large numbers of olfactory cells, which give the dog the ability to scan odors. The nose is the only part of the body where nerve tissue is directly exposed to the outside world.

In dogs, parts of the sinuses have olfactory epithelium. A puppy's sinuses are very small, but they grow as the dog grows. "The sinuses are larger when the skull is bigger," Dr. K. Wagner wrote, adding, "It looks as if this characteristic especially is bound to the searching senses."[2]

Within the sinuses, the maxillo sinus is situated directly above the mouth cavity in the same area as the roots of the teeth. As a result, infections in the upper jaw can cause infections in the maxillo sinus, affecting the dog's ability to smell. The frontal sinus, meanwhile, is in the frontal bone; olfactory epithelium are also in this cavity.

Sniffing

A dog's sniffing is an action that consists of a series of eight to 20 short puffs of inspiration followed by one expiration. During a single puff of inspiration, no turbulence—whirling of the air—is formed in the nasal cavity, as was once believed. It was thought that turbulence in the nasal cavity allowed an odor to be "scanned" more than once. In 1981, however, Dr. Walter Neuhaus stated that the space between the turbinates is too small for turbulence.[3] The small amount and low speed of the air sucked in during sniffing is below the critical value for current turbulence. Instead, the inhaled air reaches the rear parts of the olfactory mucous membrane in the sinuses by means of differences in pressure within the nose.

Due to the considerable negative pressure from behind the conchae maxillaris during inspiration, air is drawn from the spaces between the conchae ethmoidalis and from the frontal sinuses. At the end of the inspiration, scented air flows back into these spaces, so that even the parts of the olfactory epithelium located in the frontal sinuses and remote from the breathing flow are stimulated. During a single sniff, diffusion is of additional importance.

During normal breathing, the pressure difference between inspiration and expiration in the rear space of the nose is too low to transport odor molecules to the remote part of the olfactory mucosa. However, molecules diffuse effectively into the frontal

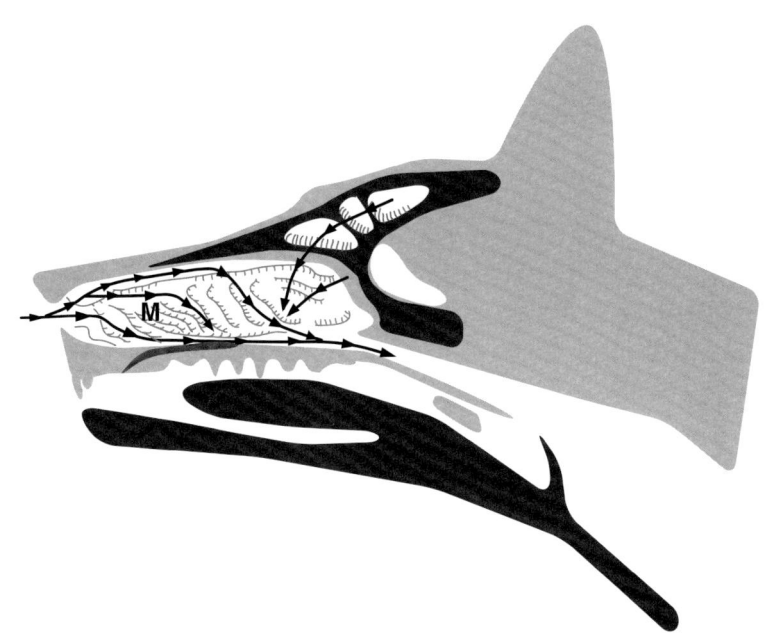

An air current moving through the dog's nose, represented by the line beginning in the nostrils. Negative pressure comes into play behind the conchae maxillaris (M). However, the air flow from the sinuses and the conchae ethmoidalis (represented by the arrowed lines coming down from the upper right) eliminates the differences in pressure.

sinus if high odor concentrations and a minimal inspiration time of two seconds are maintained.

When the dog breathes, air enters the nose through the nostrils and moves into the nasal cavity where it is warmed and moistened by the conchae maxillaris. After that, air moves through the conchae ethmoidalis, where olfactory cells scan it for odors. Then, this air may move through openings in the upper side of the nasal cavity into the sinuses where it can make contact with the olfactory epithelium.

The Vomeronasal Organ

An important contribution to the scent capacity of the dog is made by the vomeronasal organ, also called Jacobson's organ, which is present in the right and left nasal cavities. It is a small, somewhat tubular organ that begins a bit behind the upper canines and extends back over the bottom of the nasal cavity. This organ is also present and functional in humans.

In the vomeronasal organ there is an olfactory epithelium similar to that in the main nasal cavity, although the receptors are different. This organ also is able to perceive scents in addition to those perceived by the main olfactory epithelium—it can detect both pheromones and other odors—and a different part of the brain works out the messages sent by this organ that are related to these odors. In fact, the vomeronasal organ has its own nerve connection with the scent center in the brain, is open to the nasal cavity, and (by little canals) is connected to the dog's mouth.

Because it is connected to the dog's mouth, the vomeronasal organ recognizes the different odors that enter the mouth or are generated there. Many dogs lick articles to better perceive them; the vomeronasal organ can scan the smell of these licked objects. This important organ also plays a role in scent perception under water. It actually allows submerged dogs to smell objects without having to inhale.

FLEHMEN BEHAVIOR

Dogs are frequently seen licking the urine deposits of other dogs, especially those produced by bitches in heat. They chatter their teeth as they lick. After smelling or licking at certain odor sources, such as urine and other odor flags, some dogs also display what is called Flehmen behavior—also called the Flehmen response or Flehmening—a particular curling of the upper lip that facilitates the transfer of pheromones and other scents into the vomeronasal organ. Typically, dogs lift their head after contact with the odorant, wrinkle their nose, lift their upper lip in such a manner that they appear to be grimacing or smirking, and stop breathing for a moment.

The Flehmen response, which dogs adopt when examining scents left by other animals either of the same species or of prey, helps expose the vomeronasal organ and draw odors back toward it. This behavior allows dogs to detect scents, perhaps the urine of other members of their species or clues to the presence of prey. Flehmening allows dogs to determine the presence or absence of estrus, the physiologic state of the animal they are smelling, and how long ago that animal passed by.

Olfactory Cells

The olfactory epithelium looks brownish in macrosmatics (in microsmatics, such as humans, it is yellowish). The color is a result of a fat-soluble pigment in the supporting cells. The olfactory epithelium is composed of these supporting cells, basal cells, and olfactory cells.

The supporting cells—also called sustentacular cells—give general solidity to the surrounding tissue, forming an uninterrupted "soil" with little holes in which olfactory cells are confined.

In the lowest lying "soil" of the supporting cells are situated little basal cells, which can grow to become supporting or olfactory cells, replacing ones that are destroyed. The olfactory cells (also called sensory neurons or receptor cells) are similar in form to and built a lot like a primary sense cell. This type of cell, which is characteristic in lower animal forms, also occurs in the embryos of vertebrate animals and in adult vertebrates in the olfactory epithelium. These cells take in information from all kinds of gases and allow the dog to respond to what he smells in the air around him.

An olfactory cell is a bipolar nerve cell with an unbranched dendrite that terminates in an olfactory knob at the cell surface. From here, long, hair like protrusions called cilia project outwards into a layer of mucus, the mucous membrane film.[4] Receptors are thought to be located on the surface membrane of these cilia, and they form the actual scent-scan system. The axons of the olfactory

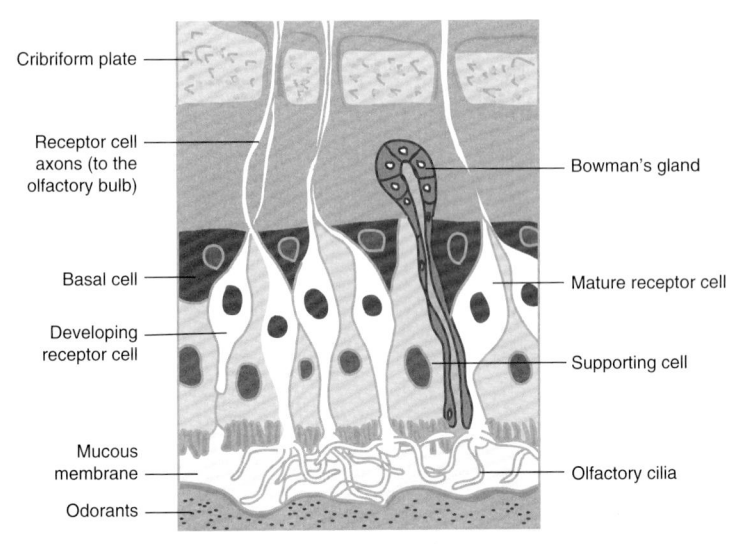

A schematic representation of the olfactory epithelium.

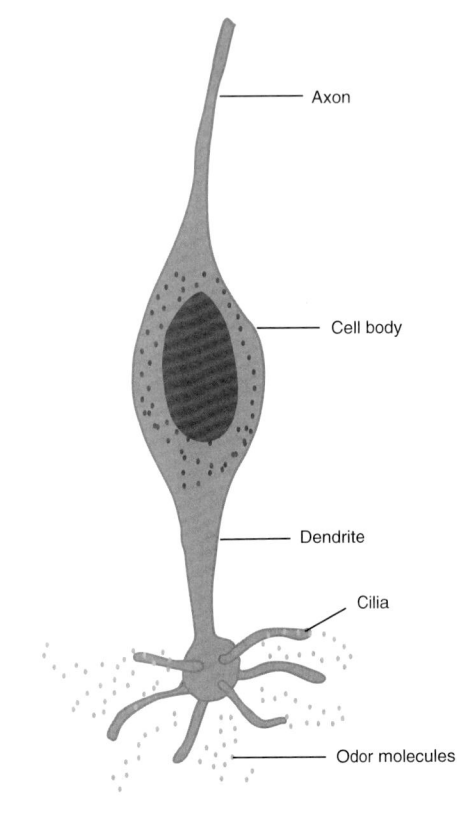

The olfactory cell. The cilia are in a mucous membrane film. The dendrites form the connections between nerves and the brain.

cells form bundles that join together to form the olfactory nerve. This nerve passes through the small openings of the cribriform plate of the ethmoid bone and terminates in the olfactory bulb of the brain. The olfactory bulb is the only region in the brain that receives direct axonal input.

Olfactory cells have a lifespan of 30 days, after which they are replaced by new olfactory cells that are produced by dividing basal cells.[5] The continuous turnover of olfactory cells means that an impairment of the sense of smell due to damaged olfactory cells is only temporary.

In humans we find between six and eight cilia per olfactory cell. The dog, according to Dr. D. Lancet, has five to 20;[6] in the opinion of Dr. J. Boeckh, up to 100;[7] and according to M.D. Pearsall and Dr. H. Verbruggen, there are 100 to 150 cilia per olfactory cell.[8] That's nothing to sneeze at.

The Mucous Membrane

The mucous membrane lining, in which the cilia are confined, is kept moist by Bowman's glands. Some of these glands produce a watery secretion, others a thick mucus. These glands cover the surface of the membrane with mucous membrane film, which affects the solubility of odors taken into the nose.

Odorous substances have to penetrate this mucous membrane film for cilia to detect them, and the mucus concentrates these odors. The mucus is complex in composition and contains many different proteins. A particular group of proteins, called olfactory binding proteins (OBP), play a very important role in facilitating contact between odors and receptors on the cilia. Odorants are generally hydrophobic but must penetrate the watery mucus to reach the receptors, and OBPs should be capable of this task. OBPs are therefore thought to have a mediating role.[9]

Olfactory Function in Dogs Compared to that in Humans

In comparison to a human, the dog has a larger surface area within his nose, as a result of the labyrinth of folds in the turbinates, and he also has a thicker mucous membrane.

A human's olfactory area is 1.6 to two inches squared (4–5 cm^2) and the thickness is 0.0002 inches (0.006 mm), so there is about 0.09 to 0.1 inches cubed (2.4–3 mm^3) of olfactory epithelium. By comparison, a medium-sized adult dog's olfactory area is 36 to 67 inches squared (92–170 cm^2) and 0.004 inches (0.12 mm) thick, which means the average dog has 43.3 to 78.7 inches cubed (1100–2000 mm^3) of olfactory epithelium. In essence, the dog is at least 260 times better equipped than the human in terms of olfactory function.

The surface of the human's olfactory area is 1/4000th of his or her total skin surface. The surface of the average dog's olfactory area (20 times thicker than that of humans) is almost the same as the surface area of his skin.

Furthermore, the average number of human olfactory cells is about 5 million, while a Teckel can have up to 125 million olfactory cells. The fox terrier has 150 million, and it is well known that the German shepherd has about 220 million olfactory cells. As well, the olfactory bulb of the dog is more than 1/3 (35 per cent)

Olfactory Function: A Comparison between Humans and Dogs

	Human	Dog	Difference
Size of olfactory area[10]	4–5 cm^2	92–170 cm^2	30x
Thickness olfactory area	0.006 mm	0.12 mm	20x
Volume of olfactory area	2.4–3 mm^3	1104–2040 mm^3	600x
Compared to total skin area	1/4000	almost total	
Number of olfactory cells[11]	5 million	125–250 million	50x
Cilia per receptor cell	6–8	100–150	20x
Olfactory bulb/total brain[12]	5%	35%	7x

of his total brain, while in humans it amounts to only 5 per cent of the brain. Although there is no known direct relationship between the size of the olfactory epithelium and sensitivity to odors, the dog's olfactory function outsizes the human's in every respect and is impressively equipped for the perception of odors.

Other Animals

The differences in the size of the olfactory epithelium among different animals are obvious when we set up comparisons, as we did above between dogs and humans. Although the size of the olfactory areas of humans and pigs is almost equal, humans have about 5 million olfactory receptor cells, while pigs have up to 300 million. That's why pigs are so good at finding truffles and are used for this purpose in France and Italy. Fish have also been found to have olfactory function that is about 250 times better than that of humans.

Mammals with excellent olfactory systems (macrosmatics) include cows, pigs, dogs, deer, hare, and rats. The latter are often used as lab animals in olfactory experiments, often related to scents perceived by the vomeronasal organ, like pheromones.

The Human's Sense of Smell

Although weak compared to that of the dog, human olfactory function is often underrated. Dr. R.W. Moncrieff proved this when he was researching extraordinarily diluted scent substances.[13] Later research by Dr. W. Neuhaus in this area also confirms that people have more ability to smell things than we give ourselves credit for.[14]

Humans actually have an extraordinary, if underappreciated, sense of smell. For example, humans can detect the scent of fear in human sweat, and they may select mates whose body odor suggests a favorable genetic makeup. Such behaviors must depend on keen olfaction. For example, the odorant ethyl mercaptan, which is often added to propane as a warning agent, can be detected at concentrations ranging between 0.2 ppb (parts per billion) and 0.009 ppb. This is equivalent to approximately three drops of the odor added to an Olympic-sized swimming pool.[15] Given two pools, a human can detect by smell which pool contains the three drops of the stuff.

Other impressive cases of human olfactory discrimination involve smells that are ecologically meaningful. For example, human participants in one study could use their sense of smell to differentiate between their own T-shirts from 100 other, identical T-shirts worn by other people for 24 hours.[16] A human mother can discriminate between the smell of her baby and that of other babies,[17] and breast-feeding babies can pick out the smell of their mothers from other mothers as early as six days after birth.[18] As Kenneth Hovis of Carnegie Mellon University, Pittsburgh, stated in 2012: "Early olfactory experience, possibly even before birth, may produce long-lasting effects in both the olfactory mucous membrane in the nose and the vomeronasal organ."[19]

Human scent detection thresholds are very low, so only unusually high odor concentrations spontaneously shift our attention to olfaction. Despite possessing a first-rate chemical detector for odors, humans appear to both underrate and mistrust it. However, many of the above-detailed human feats of olfactory discrimination were achieved despite low confidence.

Human Scent Trackers

As with dogs, humans can improve their ability to detect scents by practicing. For example, we have found that humans can learn to track a scent trail in a field, and they significantly improve their performance at this task after only four practice sessions. Jess Porter and his colleagues from the University of California, Berkeley, laid 33-foot (10-m) scent trails, including one of chocolate essential oil, in a grassy field, and they asked 32 people to find a trail and track it to the end. Those who took part were blindfolded and wore thick gloves and earplugs to force them to rely exclusively on their sense of smell.

Two thirds of the participants were able to follow the scent. And while they were slower than other animals would be while tracking the scent, their performance improved over time.[20] In other tests, it was found that humans require two working nostrils to be able to track scents.[21] Researchers have been able to prove that the human sense of smell is more powerful than was previously believed and that, with training, humans might be capable of tasks that were once thought to be the exclusive domain of non-human animals.

When meeting other dogs, the nose gives all necessary information.

5

Odors and Perception

We have tried to present the information in this book as simply as possible and to focus on aspects that are important when working with all kinds of search dogs, from tracking to scent-identification and detector dogs. Most of the scented materials these dogs train with are made up of combinations of different kinds of molecules. Some of these are light, volatile, and odorous; others are not. The "chemical" identity of a material is therefore not automatically the same as its "olfactory" identity. To prevent confusion, in this chapter we will use the term "odor" when we are talking about a material consisting of one type of odor molecules.

Do we smell the same thing our dog smells?

Sensory Organs

In general, all sensory organs work in the same way. Each sense organ has receptors. These receptors are located in or on sensory neurons. The receptors react to a signal in the environment. This signal stimulates the sensory neuron, which responds by generating an impulse. This impulse can be thought of as an electric current, running from the sensory neuron through the nerves. The impulse can be transmitted from one nerve to another until it reaches the brain, where the information the impulse carries is processed. However, problems in perception can occur along the way. Perhaps the signal cannot reach the receptor, or there is no receptor available for a certain kind of signal, or the sensory neuron does not react, or the nerve does not react, or the brain interprets the information incorrectly.

OLFACTORY EPITHELIUM

As described in the previous chapter, odor molecules can reach the olfactory epithelium by way of the nose or the mouth. The olfactory epithelium is covered with mucus, and in this mucus are the cilia that hold the olfactory receptors. Cilia are in fact extensions of the olfactory sensory neurons in the epithelium. The sensory neurons terminate in a nerve that passes through the cribriform plate—a horizontal, sieve-like bone that supports the olfactory bulb—to the olfactory bulb in the brain. In the brain, the nerves are bundled in nerve knots called glomeruli.

The density of the sensory neurons in the epithelium differs among species, and it also changes during an animal's lifetime. As a young animal grows up, the density of the sensory neurons (and corresponding sensitivity to odors) first increases; when an animal becomes really old, the density (and sensitivity) decreases.

An important and unique characteristic of the olfactory epithelium is its continuous regeneration: neurons in the epithelium live 30 to 60 days and then die, whereupon they are replaced by new neurons. Other sensory organs do not have this same ability to regenerate.

Sniffing and Air Scenting

Odor molecules float around in the air, but the odor receptors that can react to these molecules are located deep inside the nose. The main route these molecules take toward the receptors is through the nose, but odor molecules can also travel through the mouth (when an individual is eating) up through the throat to the nasal cavity and reach odor receptors in that way.

When sitting calmly, a dog breathes in and out approximately 15 times per minute. When walking calmly, the frequency rises to 31 times per minute. During such ordinary respiration, the majority of inspired air travels to the lungs via the quickest route, and odor molecules in this air do not make contact with the odor receptors in the olfactory epithelium, deep inside the nose. Only when the concentration of odor molecules is very high in the air will odor receptors be stimulated during normal breathing.

Humans and dogs must both actively sniff in order for odor molecules to reach the olfactory epithelium. When a dog sniffs, the inhalation/exhalation frequency rises from 15 to 31 to 140 to 200 times per minute. Sniffing leads to differences in air pressure in the nose, causing odor-molecule-laden air to deeply enter all the nasal cavities.

Another breathing technique that leads to scent perception has also been observed in hunting dogs, as well as in search-and-rescue dogs and other detector dogs. This technique is called "air scenting" and consists of one long inhalation—lasting 20 times longer than those performed during ordinary breathing—followed by exhalation through the mouth. This method likely leads to an optimal presentation of odor molecules to the receptors in the olfactory epithelium.

Measurements of the breathing pattern of dogs during tracking reveal that with increasing difficulty of the track, the dogs increase their sniffing frequency. The duration of the sniffing bouts also increases as track difficulty increases.[1]

ODORS AND PERCEPTION 67

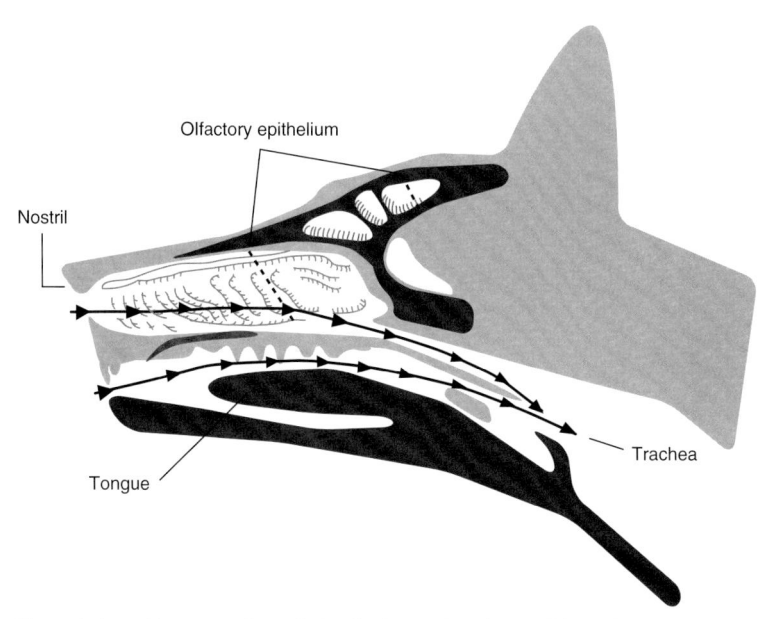

The main breathing route through the dog's mouth and nose. Taking this route, air does not reach the olfactory epithelium deep in the nose.

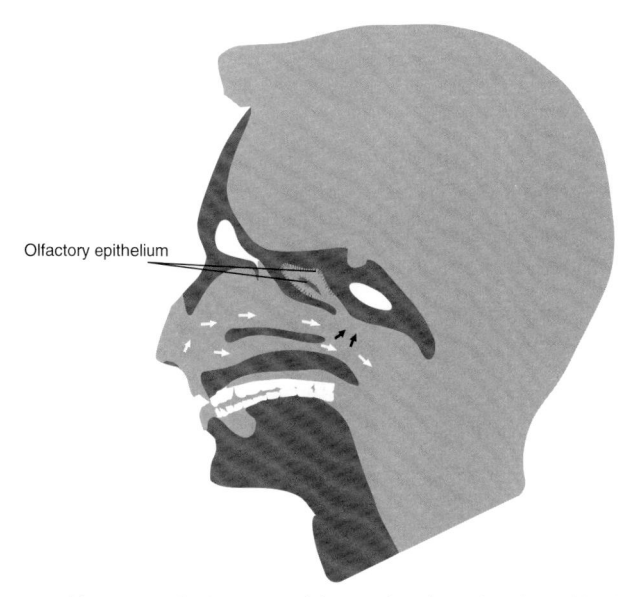

During normal human respiration, most of the air takes the path indicated by the white arrows. Only through diffusion or sniffing can odor reach the olfactory epithelium (as shown by black arrows).

Odor Receptors

The odor receptors that pick up the signals in odor molecules are located on cilia in the mucus that covers the olfactory epithelium. This mucus is watery and contains different agents that cleanse the air; for example, it contains antibodies to different bacteria, as well as detoxifying enzymes. To reach the olfactory receptors, odor molecules must first dissolve in this watery mucus, but odor molecules do not dissolve well in water.

It's a good thing that the mucus contains certain proteins (olfactory binding proteins, or OBPs) that function as carriers, aiding in the dissolution of the odor molecules. The odor molecules thus attach to these proteins, dissolve in the mucus, and are transported to the olfactory receptors located on the cilia of the olfactory sensory neurons. There are probably around one thousand different kinds of olfactory receptors, divided into at least four zones, and all dogs seem to have the same ones.[2] Consider that the eye has three different kinds of receptors (cones) that make it possible for us to see the variety of color that we do. Similarly, the tongue has receptors that allow us to experience five different tastes: sweet, bitter, salty, sour, and umami.

ONE THOUSAND DIFFERENT RECEPTORS

Every olfactory sensory neuron has several cilia with receptors. We think that all the cilia located on a single olfactory sensory neuron have the same type of olfactory receptor.[3] As we noted previously, the olfactory sensory neurons that carry the cilia and receptors live for 30 to 60 days, die, and are replaced by new neurons. At some stage during the development of a new neuron, the type of receptor it carries is determined. If a neuron with a type-A receptor, for example, dies, this does not automatically lead to the replacement neuron having the same type of receptor. Rather, the type of receptor that is generated on the new replacement neuron is (partly) triggered by the odors the animal most often smells. Wang, Wysocki, and Gold (1993), and Youngentob and Kent

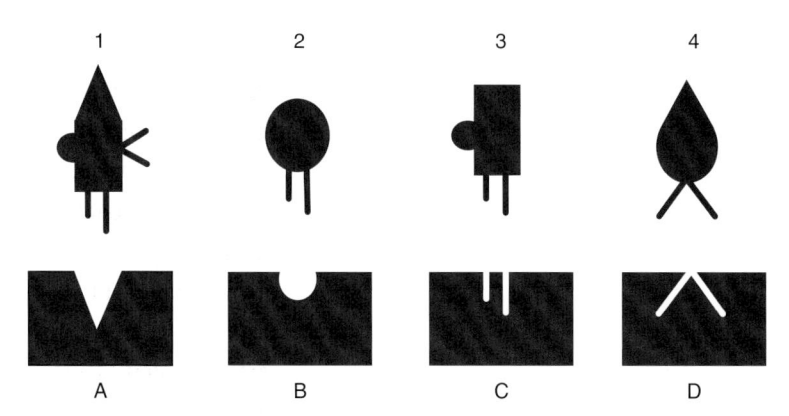

A schematic example of the relationship between odor molecules and odor receptors.
Odor 1 stimulates receptors A, B, C, and D.
Odor 2 stimulates only receptor C.
Odor 3 stimulates receptors B and C.
Odor 4 stimulates receptors A and D.

(1995) found that animals systematically trained on certain odors develop more receptors for those odors.[4]

Research thus suggests that each type of receptor reacts to a certain part of an odor molecule: a certain shape or chemical group. To simplify things for our purposes here, we will assume that part of different kinds of odor molecules is the same and as a result stimulates the same kind of receptor. However, each odor molecule also has several different parts that each stimulate different receptor types. So, a single odor will stimulate a specific group of receptor types; each odor stimulates a different group. In this way, one thousand different kinds of odor receptors can differentiate clearly amongst a large number of odors.

The precise way in which an odor signal triggers a reaction in odor receptors is unknown. In some way this odor signal leads to the firing of an impulse, which can be compared to an electric current that, once generated, is transmitted through the sensory neuron to the brain. When the presence of certain stimuli is constantly triggering certain sensory cells to fire, those cells begin to adapt to the situation. Adaptation is the adjustment of the sensory cell to weaker or stronger sensory signals. If a sensory cell is continuously stimulated in a certain way, it will cease to react to the stimulus. For example, if you enter a kitchen where cauliflower is cooking, you will immediately notice its smell, but after you spend some time in the kitchen, you won't notice it any more. If you go out of the kitchen, let your nose rest for a bit, then re-enter the kitchen, you will smell the cauliflower odor again.

Glomeruli

As soon as a receptor has reacted to an odor signal, the olfactory sensory neuron fires and an impulse is carried through the nerve to the bulbus olfactorius, the olfactory center in the brain, located directly behind the cribriform plate. The pathway between the brain and the receptor is extremely short: the sensory neuron that has the receptors on cilia at one end is the same neuron (or nerve) that delivers the impulse to the brain. Such short impulse pathways are unique to the olfactory system: in all other sensory organs the signal must be passed along to at least one other nerve—sometimes several nerves make up a pathway—before the signal reaches the brain.

Olfactory nerves converge in one to two thousand nerve-knots called glomeruli, located in the first layer in the bulbus olfactorius. The nerve ends of sensory cells that have the same type of olfactory receptor all come together in the same glomerulus. Sensory cells of a certain receptor type, therefore, have a matching glomerulus in the brain.

Because the information from many olfactory sensory neurons comes together in a single matching glomerulus in the brain, the signal is amplified in the brain. Even if only a few sensory cells are triggered by an odor, the information that odor imparts is bundled in the glomeruli and then projected in a clear signal to the mitral cells in the second layer of the bulbus olfactorius.

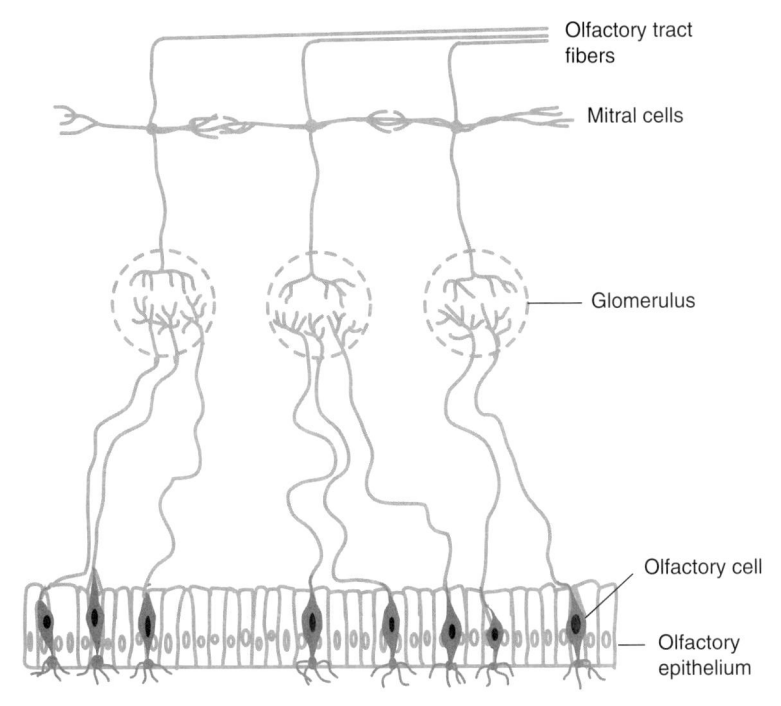

A schematic example of the relationship between the olfactory sensory neurons and the glomeruli in the bulbus olfactorius in the brain.

As previously noted, in the olfactory epithelium, sensory cells having the same receptor type are distributed evenly within a zone. Each zone in the epithelium connects with a zone in the bulbus olfactorius. Sensory cells of the same receptor type all connect to the same glomerulus. In this manner, a clear spatial pattern emerges: each odor stimulates a characteristic spatial pattern of glomeruli in the brain.

The development of the glomeruli in the bulbus olfactorius is partly determined by the kinds of odors an animal comes across most often. If you train your dog on one particular odor, for example, he will develop more olfactory sensory neurons for that particular odor, and the matching glomeruli also become more developed.

The information from the first layer of glomeruli in the bulbus olfactorius is passed on to the mitral cells, which are interconnected, leading to better perception of minute differences. This makes the signal clearer.

Cortex and Limbic System

The signals that reach the bulbus olfactorius follow two paths for further processing in the brain. One path leads to the cerebral cortex, also called "gray matter," the outer covering of the cerebrum and cerebellum. When the information imparted by the odor reaches the cortex, the animal becomes aware of the odor, knows he or she has smelled something, perhaps recognizes the odor and, if so, will react or not react to the odor. This series of events, from awareness to reaction, is called cognitive processing of information.

The other path leads deep into the brain to an area called the limbic system. The limbic system is responsible for many autonomic processes (these are independent processes we are not conscious of); it influences different physiologic processes, emotions, and sexual behavior. The limbic system receives odor information through the main olfactory epithelium and from the vomeronasal organ.

The sensory cells in the epithelium of the vomeronasal organ have different receptors than those in the olfactory epithelium of the nose. In the vomeronasal organ there are approximately 100 different kinds of receptors. Research points to this organ working in the same way the olfactory organ does: a single sensory cell has one kind of receptor, and sensory cells with the same receptor type connect to the same glomerulus in the accessory olfactory bulb (located on the dorsal-posterior region of the main bulb). Only the signals from the vomeronasal organ pass through this accessory bulb. Information from the vomeronasal organ leads, through the accessory olfactory bulb, to the limbic system of the brain.

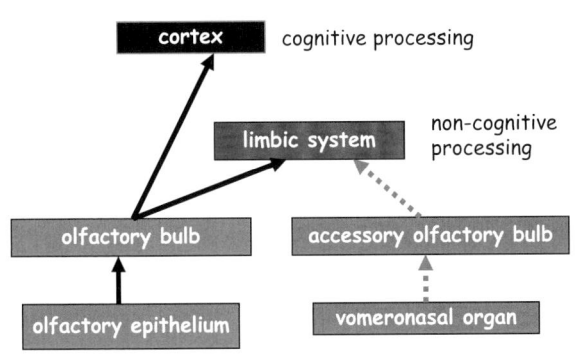

A schematic overview of the paths that olfactory information follow from the olfactory epithelium and the vomeronasal organ to the brain.

Experiments with humans have shown that even though a person's brain reacts to an odor, he or she may not be conscious of smelling something. The processing of olfactory information by the limbic system is called non-cognitive processing, meaning the person is not aware of the smell.

Odors processed by the limbic system can have great physical impact on an animal. The odor of lemons counters depression in rats. The odor of a human male shortens the menstrual cycle of a human female. The odor of a strange male leads to spontaneous abortion in a rat that has just become pregnant by another male. Some odors stimulate animals; others slow them down.

Odors Influencing Behavior

The limbic system processes information quickly, before processing happens in the cortex. This means the non-cognitive effects of odors processed in the limbic system may interfere with cognitive processing in the cortex. A good example of this taken from police practice is the reaction of a dog to the odor of a member of the kennel staff. Using the odor of this staff member as a foil in a scent-identification line-up often leads to mistakes. This can be explained by the direct, positive association the dog has with this person's odor: food, being taken for a walk, attention, praise, and so on. The dog may react to this person's odor before he "realizes" he is actually looking for a different odor. The reverse problem can also be explained in this way: an odor a dog finds "difficult" to work with may be one he has negative associations with—hence the avoidance behavior.

Another example of non-cognitive processing of odors interfering with cognitive processing is the reaction of a male dog to the scent of a female dog in heat. Her odor, as processed by the limbic system, initiates a sexual behavior pattern. Even though a dog can be taught to not follow through with the behavior, his first reaction to the odor will always be present because of his drive to procreate.

Problems with Odor

We hope that the background knowledge we have provided in the first half of this book will lead to a better understanding when problems arise as you train your dog for scent detection. First of all: many substances that are odorless for people can be perceived by dogs. Remember: everything has an odor. As well, when training your dog, consider that there are certain porous substances that can absorb and retain odors, sometimes for a long time. Many handlers have made the mistake of punishing their dogs for reacting to an odor, thinking odor was not present, only to discover later that in all probability there was an odor, perhaps in an empty hiding place. Keep in mind during training and in search situations that you can't be positive that an odor isn't present, and relatedly, remember that it's possible you and your dog might disturb or find other odors that your dog might react to.

The olfactory organ is not static; it continuously regenerates, and it reacts to differences in the environment. When an animal is confronted with a certain odor often, physical differences result in the olfactory organ. These changes can be seen on all levels: more sensory cells with certain types of receptors, larger glomeruli, and permanent changes in the brain. As well, when an animal is not in contact with certain odors, his olfactory organ will be less able to perceive them.

In general, females of a species have a more sensitive sense of smell than males. But, in both genders, sensitivity decreases with age. There are, of course, great differences among individuals, not only in people but also in other animals, such as dogs. A single individual may also differ over time, reacting with greater sensitivity at one time than at another. This can be the result of hormonal variation (among other factors). And just as one person can be sensitive, another can also be "odor blind"—some people, for example, cannot smell certain odors—a condition that is partly genetically determined.

Several illnesses influence odor perception; for dogs, the most important illness is the influenza virus. It is known that dogs that have been infected, but that do not yet show normal symptoms, already have a decreased olfactory sensitivity.

Other illnesses that can diminish the olfactory system of the dog are renal failure, hypothyroidism and, more often present in dogs, Cushing's syndrome (an adrenal hypersecretion). Problems with the upper teeth, like root infections, can also influence the dog's ability to smell. As well, certain medications, especially antibiotics, can affect odor perception.

The color of a dog's coat can also indicate his olfaction ability. Albino or pale-colored dogs' ability to smell may be diminished in part, or in full. This may explain why albino animals in the wild rarely have a chance to survive, partly because of their marked white color and partly because they are unable to distinguish odors very well.

Short-nosed breeds often experience problems with searching because of breathing problems. Boxers, for instance, can search as well as other working dogs, but they need more stops to rest.

Researchers working with scent-training animals have found that differences in the *amount* of odor appear to be perceived by the animals as differences in *kind* of odor: a lot of one odor smells

Boxers can search just as well as other working dogs, but because of the breathing problems they experience due to their short noses, they need more stops to rest.

different than a small amount of the same odor.[5] It has been established that when we perceive different amounts of odor in the air, qualitatively different processes in the brain are employed to detect those differences and translate that information.[6] Therefore, a small amount of an odor does not lead to a less strong reaction than a large amount, but to a completely different reaction. As well, it is more difficult to train an animal to discriminate between odors when they are complex (combinations of different scents) than when the odors are single odors.[7] And, if an odor is presented alone, an animal is much more sensitive to the odor than if the same odor is presented as part of a complex group of scents.[8]

Adaptation

If a sensory cell is continuously stimulated in a certain way, it will cease to react to the stimulus. Consider the cooking cauliflower example presented earlier—the same is true for dogs. When working with dogs, you may come across situations where this kind of adaptation plays a role. For example, the density of narcotic odor in a room where a lot of a certain narcotic has been hidden, or where a smaller amount has been hidden for a long time, can be intense. In a room like this, a scent-detection dog may have a hard time indicating the exact source of the odor, especially if he has been in the room for some time. The dog's sensory cells have adapted; they have been stimulated so much that they no longer react to the smell. Of course, a decrease in the magnitude of concentration of odor in such an odor-saturated environment can also explain why a dog cannot locate an odor's source.

A similar situation arises when a dog is tracking with his nose right on the surface of the track, where his sensory cells can also adapt to the track's odor. By raising his head from the track and then returning to it, he may "clear his nose" and be able to smell the scent on the track again.

We notice the same thing when a search-and-rescue dog locates a human odor, goes away from that spot, and returns more able to pinpoint the scent clue. If you punish such a dog for refreshing his sensory cells, he will not be as effective at searching and finding. Or, he will put his nose to the ground and act as though he is searching or tracking, without really doing so.

CROSS-ADAPTATION AND IRRITANTS
Another aspect of adaptation is cross-adaptation. This happens when one has adapted to a certain odor and it then becomes impossible to smell certain other odors. This phenomenon has been described for several odors, but not all cross-adaptations are known.[9]

We also know that certain chemicals—for instance, acetone and xylol—can block a great swathe of olfactory cells or push aside other scent substances. If you first smell acetone and then xylol, you can clearly perceive both odors. However, if you reverse the order, smelling the xylol first, you will find that you cannot perceive the acetone for some time.

Handlers of detector dogs especially have to be aware of this. They also must know that other substances, such as ether or benzene, can fill up the dog's nose with odor, so that it can be more or less blocked for several minutes. The dog's ability to determine finer odors becomes very difficult during that period.

Both dogs' and humans' ability to smell is also disturbed by irritants, and strong and abnormal odor prickles. Tracking on a meadow strewn with fertilizer or, for detector dogs, in a chemical-scent-laden factory or laboratory, may disturb the sensory cells. To ensure your dog can work in even such circumstances, train him on as many odors as possible and under constantly changing circumstances.

"FAILURE" ODORS

Following is an example of the relationship between smell and memory. During tests, people were given a difficult task, which they couldn't do well, and at the same time they were exposed to an unusual odor.[10] Subsequently, when asked to complete an easy, ordinary task with the same odor present, they had difficulty succeeding. The participants in this experiment had come to associate the odor with failure. Dogs, too, can inadvertently make the same connections between difficult searches and "failure" odors.

The problems some dogs encounter when searching could be connected with a "failure" odor.

Training Advice

Here are a few points you may wish to attend to as you train your dog to detect odors. The advice given below is valid for all kinds of odor-detection training. Above all, remember that it is not always possible to prevent mistakes.

1. Be aware that terms such as "odor" and "odorless" are difficult to define; use them with care.
2. Boiling an object in water is not the best way to remove odor from that object; odor molecules, after all, do not dissolve well in water. When cleaning objects, use (non-perfumed) soap or another fat-dissolving product.
3. Should your dog suffer a diminished sense of smell as a result of a damaged olfactory epithelium, remember that the sensory loss is temporary.
4. Olfactory receptors are continuously renewed, along with their olfactory sensory neurons, and they continuously adjust to the odors they perceive. So, the number of olfactory receptors for a particular odor changes according to how often that odor is smelled. Regular exposure to "training" odors leads to physical changes in the olfactory organ that increases your dog's sensitivity to these odors. Therefore, to optimize the nose of your dog, you need to provide him with continuous odor training.
5. The limbic system is the first of the sensory systems to process odor information and may influence learned behavior relative to odors. The influence of an odor on the behavior of a dog through the limbic system and possible interactions of an odor with memories can lead to all sorts of unpredictable outcomes. Try, where possible, to find out why things happen. For instance, perhaps there has been a female dog in heat that spent some time at that spot or something odorous like cheese was lying around there.
6. Odors learned when young are remembered extremely well. Begin odor training early (perhaps even in the litter) to increase your dog's effectiveness at scent detection.

Intensive search work requires all your dog's mental and physical abilities.

7. Your dog may perceive differences in amount of an odor as qualitative differences. Discriminating between complex odors is more difficult than between single odors. As well, dogs recognize a single odor in smaller amounts than when it is part of a complex compound, so training on a single odor first speeds up training on the complex odor. First train your dog on single odors, then progress to complexes of odors. Taking this route in training speeds up the learning process.

8. Be aware that differences in *amount* of odor can be perceived as differences in *kind* of odor. Train on both small and large amounts of odor, and do not expect immediate success: if your dog can find a small amount of an odor, it does not automatically mean he will also be able to find a large amount. Remember that your dog may think that a large amount of an odor is a completely different smell than a smaller amount of the same odor. When training your dog on an odor, the amounts of odor used in the training must vary. If your dog is only used to finding small amounts, he may not recognize a large amount of the same odor.

9. If an odor is presented alone, your dog is much more sensitive to it than if the same odor is presented as part of a complex of odors. This is something to be aware of in

training. Remember that if your dog is capable of finding a very small amount of a "pure" material, he may still have problems when he has to find this same small amount as part of a complex material.

10. Complex odors are learned as a unit. If your dog has previous experience with the component odors in a complex, he will learn the complex faster than if he does not have experience with the individual odors. However, a dog trained only on single odors will not always recognize these odors in complex compounds. You must train your dog both to recognize the single odors and to work out the complex compounds.

11. Be aware of the phenomena of adaptation and cross-adaptation—and adjust your training and search methods accordingly. Your dog may be unable to locate the source of a smell if the environment he is investigating is already saturated with the smell.

12. An individual's ability to smell varies over time and is influenced by such factors as hormonal variation, age, and illness. Of course, your dog's motivation to work can also vary over time. It is sensible to check your dog's capacity to smell and work: either shortly before, during, or immediately after a practical case.

6

Scent Training for Young Dogs

Your dog's sense of smell provides him with most of the information he needs about the world around him. Underestimating dogs' olfaction can lead you to ignore the enormous potential that every dog has. All dogs must use their noses to experience everyday objects and events, as well as extraordinary ones. All dogs smell the trouser legs of visitors well, and take in that odor, comparing it with other scents they already know. If smelling is so important for dogs, it would be strange not to include scent detection (searching) as part of the normal education and training of dogs. Every dog, no matter what, can search very well and likes to do it.

Searching and tracking should be a part of the normal education and training of dogs. Every dog, whether purebred or mixed, is able to search and track and likes to do it, just like this young Australian Kelpie.

For Every Dog

No dog lover should neglect searching and tracking as a part of his or her dog's upbringing. These activities provide enormous opportunities to bond with your dog and gain a better understanding of your dog's abilities. Even if you are not interested in training your dog for tracking or police tasks, if you provide your dog with an upbringing in which great attention is paid to proper training of his nose, you will afford him and yourself many advantages. Search games in dog training can double as "doggy" rewards for good practice in other areas, such as correct heeling. If your dog performs the heeling exercise correctly, for example, you can reward him by hiding his favorite ball or toy somewhere and letting him search for it. Your dog will apply great energy and excitement to the "task," and he will be extremely proud when he finds and carries away his found "prey."

Three Possibilities

Generally, there are three ways in which to stimulate your dog to search:

1. By using food as bait. Leave your dog in the care of a helper. Establish a track leading away from your dog by walking away and leaving pieces of meat or dog biscuits on the ground at regular intervals. At the end of this "track," you may also wish to lay down your dog's full food bowl. The danger inherent in this method is that your dog may

Hunting dogs and retrievers love to search for "prey," so hiding their dummy makes a fun game.

learn to pick up other food on the street or in the park that might cause illness or poisoning.

2. By using your dog's affection for you, the handler, or your family. Leave your dog in the care of a helper unknown to him. Run away and hide. Once you are hidden, the helper should release your dog, who will diligently search for you. It is important that the helper is a stranger, otherwise your dog may simply remain with the helper and not be motivated to search for you. This method is actually more suitable for an older dog than a younger one—for it to work, you and your dog must have a strong bond. Remember that presented with this situation, a somewhat insecure young dog, all alone and without the support of his handler, may panic and run away.

3. By using your dog's drive to retrieve. Hide an object that your dog really loves. Your dog will strive to find it as soon as possible and retrieve it. We do not entirely reject the first and second methods described above; however, we prefer to use this method when beginning search training. When looking for a familiar object such as a ball or toy thrown into high grass, your dog will search by pressing his nose deep into the ground; the opposite of searching with his nose held high when he searches for a person. If your dog begins searching by looking for objects, he can be taught how to search quietly and intensively because you are with him and able to guide him.

This young boxer loves to play and search for his favorite toy: a T-shirt tied in a knot.

Fetching Eagerly

In our opinion, every dog that fetches eagerly is already destined to be a good and reliable detector or tracking dog. We always start as early as possible to stimulate the retrieve drive in young dogs, so this drive can develop and be ready for training when the time comes. The more the dog properly and happily retrieves, the better and more reliable that dog later will be as a searcher or tracker. The fun of retrieving should not be underestimated. Your dog should want to retrieve—and you should also show excitement and eagerness for the game.

The exercises we think should belong in the education of every dog can be split into two categories: Bring and Search. The Bring exercise teaches your dog to quickly run after a thrown object, pick

This German Shepherd dog prefers his ball over all other retrieval toys.

This young Malinois is fond of "stolen" items, such as this umbrella.

it up, and bring it back, preferably as close as possible to you, the handler. This exercise can be taught to most dogs without pressure or undue influence.

Even before embarking on the first obedience exercises, we begin to teach every young dog (perhaps only eight weeks old) the Bring game. Almost every young dog likes to run after an object rolling along the floor to grab and play with it. To begin, try throwing a tennis ball in a sock or stocking, an old glove, or a T-shirt tied in a knot.

Bring or Fetch

Introduce the Bring game to your dog in a quiet place familiar to him. There should be no distractions. First, introduce him to the object by moving it playfully back and forth in front of his muzzle until he snaps forward and takes it. At that moment, quietly say, "Bring," or "Fetch," and then reward him by saying, "Good boy." Your dog may keep the object for a while, until you calmly say, "Out" and, with a dog biscuit under his nose, gently remove the object from him. Reward him right away with the biscuit. Repeat the exercise immediately.

Again, move the article in front of your dog's nose, and he should be interested in it. But don't let him take it immediately.

Instead, throw it a few yards in front of him, and at the same time say, "Bring" or "Fetch" in an encouraging tone. As soon as your dog grabs the object, once again clearly tell him to "Bring." Now you must make sure your young dog brings the object back to you. Get your dog's attention by making different, intriguing sounds. If he won't come to investigate those sounds, try walking backward slowly, and your dog might follow you. If he even begins to take steps toward you, reward him immediately with "Good boy, bring, good boy." Show him the dog biscuit (or other food reward) you have in your hand.

When your dog approaches you with the object in his mouth, don't just take the object from him. Say, "Bring, that's a good boy, fetch!" Then, gather your dog quietly toward you and present him with the food reward by holding the biscuit right in front of his nose. Of course, he will open his mouth for the food, so you can take the object out of his mouth, saying quietly, "Out," and then give the reward to him.

OTHER SITUATIONS

Of course, when you first start practicing the above exercise, you many encounter other scenarios. For example, your dog might grab the object and make a run for it. If he does this, he will normally bring the object to where he sleeps—his dog bed, basket, or crate. In this case, you have to use "mental pressure" to try to get your dog to bring the object to you. Next time, try throwing the object away from the place where the dog wants to bring it, in such a way that he will have to pass you on his way to that place. As he passes by, you can gently hold him, or gently take the object. Make sure you do this calmly as you say, "That's a good boy, fetch," and show him the food reward.

If you practice at home, you can also throw the object into a room that your dog usually is not allowed to enter. Once you've thrown the object and your dog has gone into the room to fetch it, kneel in the doorway so that you can receive your dog, who will want to go back into the "known" room after he has retrieved the object. You can also perform this exercise in your backyard or in another place that is closed in.

If your dog brings the object to a place in front of you and drops it there, that's still a good start for a beginning dog. In this case, pick up the object, show your dog his food reward, and then give it to him. After this, the game starts again. Always be ready to show your dog the food reward as he approaches you with the object in his mouth.

If your dog has a passion for this exercise, he may fetch and bring the object right back to you, sometimes even sitting in front of you and giving the object to you, almost as a dog might be required to do for an obedience test. Express your satisfaction with him by rewarding him, petting him, and saying, "Good boy." However, do not be tempted to enforce any test requirements, because your dog should always enjoy retrieving.

On that note, it is important for you, the handler, to know how many times you can repeat this game before your dog loses interest. You must not repeat to the point where your dog is no longer having fun—you definitely know you've gone too far when your dog stops the game all by himself. In such cases, never force him to continue the game. We advise you to stop the exercise after four to five repetitions, and only take the game up again after a few hours' respite.

The Bring exercise for the young dog may be called successful if your dog, with no other pressure than the words "Fetch" or "Bring," runs quickly to the thrown object and quickly retrieves it close to you. As soon as your dog understands the exercise, you can change the working site and also the sort of object you throw. For example, young dogs don't mind picking up keys. By using keys as a retrieve object, you can both add variety to the game and get your dog used to picking up metallic objects, which older dogs often do not want to pick up and retrieve.

As you progress, throw the objects farther and farther away, and you can stop tantalizing your dog with the object before the retrieve, too. If you notice that your dog isn't interested in fetching, however, go back to waving the object in front of his nose and exciting him with it before throwing it.

Searching for Objects

As your dog begins to retrieve reasonably well, you can boost his drive to retrieve by combining the Bring exercise with Search for the Object, which you will have hidden somewhere. Note that this combination of exercises can at first be problematic if you don't clearly teach your dog that he needs to search. When you hide the object, making sure your untrained dog isn't looking, and then expect him to search, your dog will not know what to do. In fact, he will do everything except search. After watching your dog flounder around for a while, you might attempt to bring him over to where the object is hidden, but at this point you will both feel frustrated, and a misunderstanding will arise between the two of you. During his short life, your dog has probably already heard you grumble, and that grumbling was always accompanied by something unpleasant. Your grumbling during this exercise may make your dog come to the following understanding: My handler is grumbling because of the object; searching for that object is not allowed. Without knowing it, you have created a barrier between your dog and the object. It may be possible to overcome this barrier, but somewhere in the dog's mind there will always be an inhibited feeling about the exercise and the object, which may translate into him never reaching the highest achievements in this area.

To make it clear to your dog that he has to search for the hidden object, you have to work with him carefully. An article lying on the ground somewhere, not moving, will not inspire your dog to hunt; a moving object, however, is immediately an exciting prize for him. Remember that your dog was originally a hunter, and everything that moves quickly will be recognized as prey and activate his hunting drive. Therefore, the first few times you teach him this Search exercise, throw the object some yards in front of him, into grass that is rather tall, and immediately give him the commands "Search" and "Fetch." Your dog already knows "Fetch," so if you say that after commanding, "Search," he will quickly learn to understand the "Search" command. If you follow these steps, your dog will almost always immediately and diligently seek for his beloved object.

Once the object disappears in the tall, thick grass—and there is no track to the object—your dog's search drive will kick in. The search drive is instinctive, inherited by your dog from his forebears; it is not necessary for him to "learn" to search. What your dog will learn through this exercise, by searching for play prey, is to use his sense of smell very intensively. Besides this, he may also gain some experience in catching odors on the breeze and therefore figure out how to exploit air turbulence in order to find odor traces, which is very important for his future work as a search dog.

While he is searching for the object, you may not help him in any way. Your dog has to find the object all by himself, otherwise during difficult searches your dog may wait until you help him or bring him to the place of the hidden object, and that, of course, is not correct. Instead, while your dog works at searching and locating, watch him; take this opportunity to learn to understand your dog's body language and search behavior.

As soon as your dog has found the object, he will pick it up and carry it around, full of pride. For him, this article is real prey. Now you can interfere by repeating the command "Bring" and finishing the exercise by offering your dog praise and a food reward.

Continuing Exercises

If your dog is finding his thrown object at a short distance, you can increase his passion for the search by stepping it up a bit. Go to a meadow that has high grass or a fallow, overgrown piece of land. Play for a while without asking him to search for the object, then ask your dog to lie down, or tie him to a tree. Walk away through the meadow with the object in hand, visible or not. Your dog must stay quiet. Take many steps and cross over your own track a few times so you leave no scent trail for your dog, and then drop the object in a bush or a clump of grass. All the while, your dog should be watching you. After you drop the object, continue walking in a zigzag pattern for a while, and then go back to your dog. Here, you will usually discover that your dog is already looking very interested in the meadow and is full of "search fever." Let your dog smell your hands and then give the command "Search."

If this goes well, in subsequent practices you can try dropping the object in the grass or bush without your dog seeing. During these exercises where you do not throw the toy, you can see whether or not your dog has been searching for the object (both now and when you threw the toy) with his nose. If not, that is, if he has been searching with his eyes up until now, he may have trouble searching for the hidden object. In spite of that, you should not help him. Your dog will learn best by trial and error—he has to solve this problem all by himself. Should he give up his search and look at you from afar, command, "Search," again in a friendly tone, and add, "Fetch."

If your dog finds the object without a problem, only repeat the game two or three times. Gradually, in subsequent practices, you can make the object more and more difficult to find: choose a more difficult place in which to hide the object, or practice the search game in other places and in different situations.

Remember to always show your dog your empty hands before he begins his search, and allow him the opportunity to extensively sniff your hands, too. After a while, however, you will notice that your dog knows your odor so well that he doesn't need to smell your hands before searching for the object. Another thing to remember about this exercise, and all Search exercises, is that it should end with some regular ball and Bring games that don't involve searching, so that your dog comes away from the experience relaxed and happy.

When you discover that your dog is looking very interested in the meadow—with an expression much like that of this young German shepherd—and is full of "search fever," let him smell your hands and command him to "Search."

The First Track

In these first retrieve and search exercises, you have taught your dog to retrieve and search in a pleasurable environment. You can also make tracking a fun game for your dog if you give him a lot of freedom and work with him easily, not applying any pressure. By doing this, you are preparing your dog for subsequent training in scent identification, tracking, and all other kinds of search work.

The basics of tracking begin with your dog following human footprints to find his beloved retrieving object. Any dog can do this properly—and they always have fun doing it, as long as you set the exercise up in the right way.

Your dog should have already learned to Bring and Search, and should be somewhat accustomed to waiting for the next exercise.

As well, woodland, grassland, or cropland must be available to you as terrain for the tracking exercise, and there must be a place on the terrain where your dog can quietly wait. You can always bring a corkscrew dog tether with you to the terrain if there isn't anything there to which you can fasten your dog. Such tethers, when securely screwed into the ground, allow your dog to be safely fastened, and their revolving attachments for the leash ensure that your dog will not get tangled up.

The tracking object we prefer to use is one that is not too big and not too brightly colored, something that our dog likes to fetch. To begin, bring your dog into the right mood for tracking by having him peacefully fetch this object two to three times. Then, secure your dog to the tether, or a tree, calmly say, "Wait," show him the retrieving object, and walk backward away from him. Your dog will stay attentive and observe what happens. After walking backward for about 33 feet (10 m), stop and toss the object with more flair than usual, making sure your dog is watching when it falls down. Now, walk quickly, following a big arc away from the track and back to your dog, praise him, and give him the already well-known command, "Search." Of course, your dog will now diligently search for the object.

If during this first time out your young dog does not discover that the fastest way to the object was following your footsteps, you can help him the next time by pointing to the track and motivating him with "Search, good boy" to follow your track to the object. While doing this, you can sniff clearly and audibly, which will increase your dog's interest in sniffing.

When your dog finds the object, reward him enthusiastically, "Good boy, search," and encourage him to bring it to you with the command "Fetch." But "Fetch" should hardly be necessary if you have already taught your dog in a playful way to retrieve in all kinds of Search games. When your dog approaches you with the object, quickly reverse back to the place where he was tied up, encouraging him to keep coming to you with "Bring, good boy."

This dog is interested in the smell of human footsteps.

When he arrives, reward him well and take the object from him, giving him some dog biscuits in return.

Follow up by repeating the exercise a couple of times, using the same track. Remember that your dog must first understand that after you say "Search," you expect him to go to the object, making use of your footsteps. After a break of half an hour, you can repeat the exercise in other places. Don't train too long or too often in succession, though, or your dog will cease to find fun in the exercise or, even worse, begin to dislike it.

The Dog Is Not Confused

A question we are frequently asked about the command "Search" is "How can you give your dog exactly the same command for three things: to search for the hidden object, for scent identification, and for tracking? Will that not confuse the dog?" Such questions underestimate the dog's amazing ability to search and observe. Your dog is not stupid, and he knows exactly how he must work out the three different exercises, despite the single command.

Consider that you first taught your dog that the command "Search" meant he had to find a thrown object by using his nose to sense the drift of smell. He has also learned that he should first smell the ground, because a track brings him more quickly and easily to the object. If after learning about the track the dog is once again asked to find something without a track of footsteps to guide him, well, initially he will try to find a track; if that fails, he will usually be even more determined to find the object, and he will put his nose in the air and try to smell his object. If you have trained your dog to search independently, to use his nose well, he will figure out a way to find his object.

We have a practical example of a difficult search that shows just how "unconfused" dogs are by the command "Search," and just how innovative they can be in difficult circumstances. One afternoon, we were called in to help find a runaway child. The search area was cluttered, and we arrived at the scene with our dog after several hours had already passed. We commanded our dog to "Search," and he tried to find a track in the surrounding area, but it was impossible. There had already been too many people searching for the child in the area.

We didn't have to say a word, however, before our dog put his nose in the air and tried, like a hunting dog does, to receive an odor. We walked a long way through the terrain, and suddenly he sensed something by way of his nose—he started running. He found the child's pullover and brought it to us. Then, he went back to his search. At some point, another scent came his way: he tracked that scent, lost that track, but then again went back to searching with a high nose. In this way, after a few miles, and now in the dark, he found the sleeping child. Our dog came back to us and by his conspicuous behavior made it clear that he had discovered something. He whined softly and ran in a certain direction, always looking back to make sure we were following. Sure enough, he led us to the place where the child was sleeping in the forest.

Well, if this dog had needed a different command for each of his actions, he wouldn't be a dog! You see, the whole series of actions are part of a whole: *Go, search; near the bushes you find a sweater; bring it to your boss; start a new search; find a track; walk that track; lost; search the terrain with a high nose; catch the scent again and follow it; before you there lies a human; go tell your boss.*

What influence would a series of different commands—maybe "Track," "Look for human," and "Search and help"—have had on these operations? Obviously none. The only influential command the handler can speak is at the beginning of a search action. All other commands the dog receives himself from the terrain he is searching; what he finds along the way determines his course of action. Of course, the dog must have already and thoroughly learned the separate elements of searching before such a complicated search, and he and his handler must also have a strong bond.

Thus, your command only serves as the initial prickle to start a search, and for that the spoken words are of no importance. And so, we always say that when a dog is being asked to use his nose, you only need to utter the command "Search."

Quietly Building Up to the Next Step

By this point, your young dog now shows interest in your footprints and also notes that following your footprint track is the fastest way to his beloved object. The more your dog understands the exercise, the less help you give. You can stop walking backward to create the track now, and you don't have to toss the object, but just let it fall down in front of you, walk a few steps more, then turn around and trace a wide arc back to your dog.

Remember to pay attention to the wind direction when practicing tracking. Allow your dog to search for his object against the wind (with a headwind) in the beginning so he can find it easily, but later get him to search with a crosswind and then a tailwind. These different wind directions have different influences on the track and corresponding effects on the way your dog uses his nose.

Tracking against the wind makes tracking easy for the dog, but it also entices him to search superficially, with a high nose. Crosswinds give the dog experience in searching beside the track but can bring his nose up and encourage him to be, just as in searching against the wind, a "high-nose" seeker. Dogs that already tend to seek with a high nose should not train too often against the wind or with crosswinds.

When your dog is working with a crosswind, you can observe how he uses his nose. Throw, for example, a light object at the end of a crosswind-buffeted track, and allow it to be carried by the wind to its resting place. By assessing the width of the throw, you can evaluate how well your dog uses his nose on the track.

Tailwind tracking—depending on the strength of the wind—is usually the most difficult for dogs. Tailwinds force dogs to bring their noses close to the track and to track slowly—good practice for dogs that like to seek with high noses.

A Passion for Searching and Tracking

The education of your young dog prepares him for his subsequent training. A good education will make that training easier. Make sure early tracking training does not include any pressure. Know that training your young dog according to the described method could easily teach your dog to superficially search, which is actually wrong. But, if you first teach your dog the core of each exercise, you will train him well. Only after teaching the core of the exercise do you go into the details and the correct technical execution. The core of searching and tracking exercises lies primarily in generating the desire to search and to track. At this stage, your dog's track and search drives should not be limited—later training of all the details may possibly bring in conscious or unconscious compulsion. Coercion in training will always make your young dog feel uncomfortable, especially if you apply direct constraints, such as a leash or long line. The leash or long line is a palpable force, and so it should not be used when teaching a young dog. The young

Give your young dog unrestricted access to the search area at first so that he can fully experience it and become crazy about searching and tracking.

Never forget that during training with young dogs, such as these two Bouviers des Flandres, there should always be enough time to play.

dog must feel free and unrestricted when he searches and tracks, so that he can have an optimal experience of these activities and become crazy about searching and tracking, which he naturally can already do so well.

To limit superficial tracking habits in your young dog, make sure the tracks you create are not too long; first 67, then 164 to 328 feet (20, then 50 to 100 m), are more than long enough for the first few months of learning. Moreover, no tracks should be laid without some turns. The turns teach the dog to search through different wind directions, which is natural and normal for dogs, anyway. All of these safeguards should ensure your dog tracks slower and with a deep nose. We emphatically warn against offering young dogs a long and straight track. Nothing shapes a young dog into a superficial searcher more than a monotonous, long, straight track on which there is nothing interesting for the dog to do.

Another way to make your dog track slowly is to place objects or articles on the track: the first article immediately after 33 to 49 feet (10 to 15 m), the second 98 feet (30 m) away, and the third after another 164 feet (50 m). Initially, only lay down two, and later three or more articles on the track. Walk slowly after your tracking dog, let him retrieve an object, and then quietly encourage him to continue tracking and find the other objects.

Note that you must ensure that your dog is not bothered by wind as he tracks, either sweeping in on him from the rest of the track or from other tracks nearby.

It bears mentioning again that you should never help your dog work out the track or with difficulties, as at a turn. Your dog should be able to find the correct track and hold it.

As your young dog learns to search and track, his pleasure (and your own) is the most important factor. Working correctly should only come into the training later, when your dog is older. First, your young dog must become a fan of searching and tracking, and gain a true passion for the exercises.

7

Training Scent-Identification Dogs

There are several methods you can use to teach your dog to perform at a scent-identification line-up. In the book *K9 Suspect Discrimination* by Adee Schoon and Ruud Haak (Brush Education, Inc.), the authors present a technical method for teaching dogs how to discriminate amongst different scents in a line-up. In this chapter, however, we will tell you how we have always been able to teach our service dogs to successfully negotiate such line-ups.

Before you begin, your dog should already be able to retrieve on command. (See the previous chapter for the steps involved in teaching this important step.) Young dogs are easily tempted to chase moving objects, particularly a thrown ball. And they soon find out that if they retrieve the ball, they can play the game again. If you combine this retrieval game with commands, your dog will soon know what the commands mean.

Sort and Track

The sorting out of objects also plays an important role in tracking training. A lot of people have difficulty in teaching their dogs to track, even though searching and tracking are the most natural things in the world for dogs. Dogs live in a world of odor, and they use their sense of smell always and everywhere.

Usually people first train their dogs to track and then teach them to work out scent-identification line-ups. This is not the right way to do it: the dog must first learn to search and then to track. Before the sort can be taught, the dog must have learned what "Search" means. And, indeed, the best, fastest, and most enjoyable way for the dog to learn "Search" is to play a variety of search games and work out simple tracks, as we described in the previous chapter.

Once the dog knows "Search," and he can search for and retrieve an object, possibly by making use of a track, he is able to learn scent identification. But as you train the sorting exercises, the previously learned search games and tracking should not be neglected.

Favorable Circumstances for Training

For your dog to achieve fine results in scent-identification line-ups as well as in tracking, you must teach him the various exercises in an order that is systematic and logical from your dog's perspective. A dog can learn tracking or sorting out of smells and objects well only if conditions are favorable. These favorable conditions may be specified thus:

1. The dog must be sufficiently obedient.
2. The handler must fully realize that the dog—not the handler—is the "searcher."
3. The handler should be aware that the dog is not a "universal" aid, but a very special individual that can serve only under favorable conditions.
4. The handler must be convinced that the dog gives us valuable clues, which humans must then work out and interpret.

Preliminary Sorting Exercise

To teach your dog scent identification, start with the easiest possible exercise. For a novice dog, the exercise should meet the following requirements:

1. The exercise should be done with a single scent: that of the handler; only one odor should be present on the objects presented to the dog.
2. The exercise should be easy to verify.
3. The exercise should be so easy that the dog can perform it without any help from the handler.

We call this exercise the Preliminary Sorting exercise, although this designation is factually incorrect because it has nothing to do with actual scent-identification line-ups. Indeed, no dog will have a problem picking out the objects that are drenched in his handler's odor.

Practice Is Important

For service dogs, practicing scent-identification exercises are important, sometimes more important than tracking human footsteps. The sorting exercise allows dogs to show that they can recognize an arbitrary amount of odor on an object; gradually we can change that amount of odor to see how the dogs react. How much we can vary the amount of odor on an object and still observe our dogs demonstrating their understanding of the odor is impossible to say in advance. It all depends on the level of co-operation between the dog and his handler and on the boundaries to the individual dog's sense of smell.

Scent identification allows us to be able to check on our dogs' olfaction ability in an exact way and to acclimate our dogs to the idea of working systematically. Scent-identification training can further form an excellent foundation for tracking dogs. After all, working out the track on the ground is basically nothing more than the sorting of smells.

Conditions

Learning scent identification has its problems. First, the act of sorting presupposes the presence of several types of odors, and it is not always possible to find enough people to help you provide enough different odors. Furthermore, handling the already-scented objects is a bit difficult, but you can solve this problem by moving the objects using pliers or tongs. In addition, it is not possible for your dog to search until you give him well-defined instructions. In this case, that instruction must be: "Here is a certain smell. Now, find the corresponding odor."

It is a known fact that dogs are able to remember odors. As we humans recognize people we have not met for a long time by seeing their faces and consulting our brains, so a dog recognizes something by smelling it and then consulting his memory. Recognition happens because the dog has formed an "image" of the odor in his mind. Every dog handler has experienced how his or her dog behaves when a household member comes home after a long absence. This family member's smell may stir up pleasant memories in the dog, which may cause the dog to become somewhat giddy. As well, that family member will need to submit him or herself to the dog for a thorough sniffing, so that the dog can find out—by consulting the odors he encounters and his memory of those odors—where that person has been.

As the handler, it is your duty to make sure your dog knows that odors are necessary for searching, tracking, and sorting. He must learn to inhale a given odor and, when he smells it again somewhere, be able to follow its track or to retrieve or alert you to an object with that odor. This is difficult, but it is necessary for our tasks. A dog that is insufficient in picking up an odor can never be a good searcher or tracker because that dog does not know the task he must perform.

To train scent identification well, you must accustom your dog to a certain habit, which he will pick up by doing the same thing over and over again. This habit is linked to a specific command uttered by you, the handler. After some time, when you say the command, your dog will perform the action.

Giving Scent

When giving scent to your dog, work as follows. Give your dog the well-known command "Down." Now, place an object of sufficient size—a leather wallet or a leather glove—on the floor between his forelegs. This object should have been in contact with human odor for some time, at least a half hour in your pocket, for example. Note that you should regularly use different kinds of objects, but don't discount reusing an object from time to time.

When you first do this, your dog, curious, will likely bring his nose to the object. Make sure the object lies on the floor in such a way that the better part of it is available to your dog for sniffing. If you do this, your dog will be able to fully take in the odor emanating from the object. He will smell your odor and recognize it.

Now, gently lay your hand on your dog's head and say in a calm and encouraging tone, "Smell." Of course, you can use another word, just as long as you always use the same one.

After some time, say half a minute, take the object away and release your dog's head. Reward him with your voice and caresses. Wait about half a minute and then repeat the steps: place the object down, slowly and gently press your dog's head down to just above the object, and say "Smell."

The first time the dog encounters the object, he will certainly not consciously smell it. He smells it unconsciously, as is customary with every object that comes within his reach. However, after a few times, your dog will understand that there is something special going on: "Hey, there's that same smell again."

When using this method, we have noticed that dogs learn to pick up the odor on objects very well, especially when, after pronouncing "Smell," we ourselves intensively sniff, making loud sniffing noises. When you sniff, you encourage your dog to do the same.

Present the object in this way about three times in succession, no more than four times in one sitting, though, or you risk

TRAINING SCENT-IDENTIFICATION DOGS

A short-haired Dutch Shepherd searching a scent line-up.

A modern scent line-up with metal tubes on a platform.

resistance on the part of your dog. Your dog should enjoy this exercise, so make sure you let him know how satisfied you are with his work. Always remember that your dog learns best when you mostly give rewards and encouragement, not when you always dish out punishment.

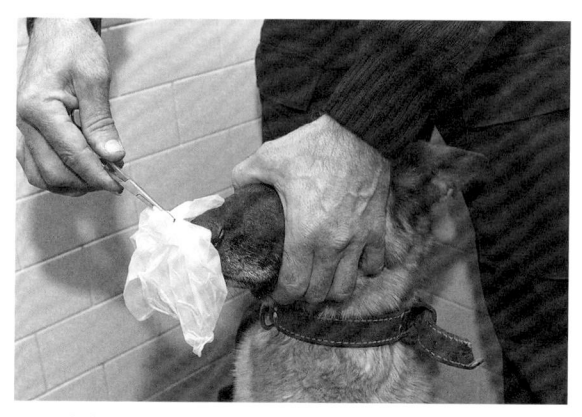

Instead of this method for giving scent, it is better for service and working dogs to learn to independently move their head toward indicated objects (or footprints, for that matter) to take in the scent.

Allow your dog to move his own head toward the object instead of raising the object to his nose. This independent movement is not only more in agreement with your dog's nature—he usually moves his head toward objects, after all; objects rarely rise to meet his nose—but it is also important because in practice it is often impossible to bring an object up to our dogs' noses. Think about foot or handprints on the ground or on window frames, door handles, and the like. Your dog must get used to hearing the command "Smell" and bringing his nose to whatever you indicate.

Sometimes you have to give your dog the scent in the open air, in which case it is best to situate the object in such a way that the wind blows in the direction of your dog's nose. The wind then blows over the largest part of the object and enters his nose, giving him a good whiff of the object's smell.

Of course, for this exercise you don't have to wait for a strong wind in order for your dog to take in the scent. Your dog's olfaction is so excellent that you don't have to worry. However, make it clear what you expect from your dog. For many dog handlers, this clear communication is the biggest challenge.

Introductory Exercises

In principle, the various exercises related to scent identification fall into two categories: the introductory exercises and the exercises in the sort. The introductory exercises aim to get the dog used to the procedure followed during sorting. These exercises should be very simple, and the dog should perform them accurately. Before you begin implementing these exercises, however, you need some accessories: wooden batons, an object belonging to you, pliers or tongs, and a closable metal box.

In the introductory exercises, we always begin by using a wooden baton because the dog can easily pick it up and it feels pleasant in his mouth. During the first round of introductory exercises, we recommend that you have at least 20 wooden batons, each of them about one by one inch (3 × 3 cm) and about five inches (12 cm) long, as well as an object belonging to you, such as a wallet or leather glove. Furthermore, make sure you have some pliers or tongs, which allow you to easily move the wooden batons; a clean metal tin or lunchbox with a lid that closes properly; and a simple rope or wire net.

You can cut up and shape your own wooden batons, or have someone do that for you. When they are ready, make sure they are hung up in a dry, cool place so that they might become as scent-free as possible—of course, they will always have the scent of wood on them. After using them, or before using them for the first time, we place the batons outside under an overhang in the wire/rope net, leaving them there for about four days in the fresh air. After that, they will not have much odor attached to them, except for the basic scent of wood, making them suitable for our purposes.

If you don't have a good place at which to train in the immediate vicinity of the overhang, use your pliers to remove the batons from the net and put them in the clean tin container, then seal it carefully. In this way you can transport your practice tools without other odors affecting the batons. Put at least 12 batons into the tin, and put five others into your pocket, ensuring they are there for at

Use pliers or tongs to pick the batons up and lay them on the ground.

least a half hour before you practice. Remember to put your wallet or glove into your pocket, too.

When you arrive at the training area, ask your dog to lie down in a convenient location. Then, use the pliers to remove between six and eight batons from the tin container. A caution here is certainly necessary: when removing the batons and putting them in, make sure your hands and body do not touch them. Always use the pliers when handling them, and always use a clean tin when transporting them.

When you have extracted the batons, put them in a straight row, one after the other on the ground, leaving a space of about 20 to 24 inches (50–60 cm) between them. Make sure your dog has a tail wind while sorting.

Now, take one of the batons out of your pocket and put it on the ground. Make sure you place it a considerable distance away from the batons in the "line-up" and that your dog can see you as you do so.

Next, give your dog the scent by placing the wallet or glove in between his forelegs, as described previously. Do this in such a way that your dog has his head in the wind, so opposite to the line-up. After you have given him the scent, bring your dog into the vicinity of the baton that had been in your pocket and give him the command "Fetch" or "Search." Without hesitation, your dog will retrieve the scent-laden baton and after you give the command "Out," you can take it from your dog with your hands. Never forget to reward your dog with praise and caresses. When he is rewarded this way, he knows he's done his job well.

If your dog does not directly retrieve the baton, encourage him to do so. You may need to return to the retrieving exercises, making sure he learns how to retrieve on command, but in a different training place.

An Attractive Baton

When you ask your dog to retrieve the scented baton, you are doing two things: first, you are asking him to be attentive to his work; and second, you are making the baton more attractive to him, since he now has had it in his mouth. Not only does this baton have the handler's odor on it, it now also has the dog's odor on it.

When you have taken the baton from your dog's mouth, place it about a half-yard in front of the line-up. Again, give your dog the scent, and then point at the row of batons and give the command "Fetch."

The first baton your dog comes across is the one with the familiar odors. He should pick it up without hesitation and retrieve. Reward him for his good work when he brings the baton to you.

The next step is to put the odorous baton in the second position in the line-up. However, do not simply exchange the odorous baton for the one in the second position, for, the place where that baton has been lying now has an odor on the ground, which could set your dog off on a wrong track. Instead, use your pliers to move the line-up so it is at least half a yard away from the original spot. Place the odorous baton in the second position with your hands, and position the rest with the pliers.

Now, give your dog the scent from your wallet or glove, and then send him to the line-up to fetch the correct baton. He will

After taking in the smell of an object, this dog went to work to find and retrieve the wooden baton with the corresponding odor.

likely find the correct baton and bring it back. The next step is to rearrange the line-up again, so that the baton is in a place farther down the row; keep doing this until the odorous baton is in the last position in the line-up. When you notice your dog skipping over batons to get to the one he knows is "right," repeat the exercise with the odorous baton at the beginning of the line-up, and build up the exercise again.

The exercise can be regarded as successful if your dog is picking up the correct baton wherever it is in the line-up, after smelling all the previous batons. If your dog goes along the row but does not retrieve the baton, call him back gently and quietly, and give him more time to smell the wallet before sending him back to the line-up again. Under no circumstances should you allow your dog to wander off in a different direction.

Working Independently

Why do we recommend training scent identification in this way?

First, we want the dog to work independently and without influence from the handler—but we don't want him to go his own way and more or less "accidentally" perform the exercise. Rather, working in this way, you, the handler, are forced to encourage your dog to work independently. In the real world, only the scent-detection dog is qualified to identify objects by scent. There is no instrument comparable to the nose of the dog, and so you, the handler, should be entirely guided by your dog. Remember that you should not intervene because you lack the power to correct your dog in a real-life exercise. We could not, for example, have helped our dog find the sleeping child we mentioned in the previous chapter—he had to do that work by himself. Giving your dog the independence he needs, right at the beginning of training, teaches him from the start that he must do his job alone.

To achieve this independence, the exercises must be as easy as possible at first. Really, it must be impossible for the dog to make a mistake. This is why, before the first introductory exercise, you ask your dog retrieve the odorous baton, adding his own odor to the already scent-laden object. The risk of mistakes happening is thus minimized. Once the dog is familiarized with this baton with the double odor, the next step is to have him find a baton on which only the smell of his handler can be detected. This very gradual increase in difficulty is only implemented when you are sure your dog is ready, so you must watch him carefully to ensure he is ready for this step up in the training.

Second, you, the handler, should refrain from interfering in your dog's work. You should not influence him while he is working by uttering words of approval or disparagement, or by making gestures. After all, if your dog notices that when his nose is above the proper baton the words "Good boy" are spoken, he may hover over the batons next time waiting for your words. If you aren't careful, you can have a strong influence on the choices your dog makes in the line-up. Be guarded in your behavior—your dog is a very fine observer. Once your dog shows some skill in sorting out the scent line-up, monitor his progress by having a helper arrange the batons into the line-up, out of sight of both you and your dog.

Just as "Good boy" can influence your dog's sorting behavior, the word "No" can also have repercussions. As soon as your dog hears this, he will sense dissatisfaction or even punishment. Suppose your dog picks up the wrong baton to retrieve and he hears "No." Your dog will be tempted to immediately drop that baton and may draw the conclusion that the retrieving itself gave rise to the penalty. Next time, he might be anxious when retrieving or even refuse to make a choice. In short, after hearing "No" in this context, your dog will no longer be able to imagine what is expected of him and will nervously walk back and forth, a very undesirable behavior at a line-up.

Choosing the Wrong Object

Just to refresh, following is the proper order of commands and praise in this exercise. As you give your dog the scent, you should say "Smell." Then you should command, "Fetch," or "Search," and if the correct baton is retrieved and brought to you, you should praise your dog with gusto.

Should your dog retrieve the wrong baton, take little note of it, tap the baton gently, and say, "Out." Don't pick the baton up with your hands. Your silence should indicate to the dog that this was not the right baton, and at the same time silence does not pass along anxiety or fear to your dog. Give your dog the scent again, giving him plenty of time to sniff the wallet, and then send him back to the line-up.

If he makes an error again, ask yourself why this is happening. We have noticed that when this happens, it is often because the exercise was not built up correctly, and the dog may not understand what is expected of him. Perhaps you, the handler, are placing pressure on your dog without knowing it, and to satisfy you, your dog is simply picking up an arbitrary baton to retrieve.

Alternatively, perhaps your dog is older and he is used to retrieving every object, whether or not it has an odor on it. In this case, a new factor emerges: how do you teach your dog to sniff objects before picking them up? As always, there are ways to train this desirable behavior.

First, you can bring your dog into an environment where he is not accustomed to working and where he is not distracted, so he pays more than ordinary attention to the objects he has to retrieve. The exercise can be done in the hallway of a house, in an attic, in a room, or another place where your dog is not distracted. This change of scenery will help many dogs improve their performance.

Another way is to prickle your dog's curiosity by using objects he has never seen before in the line-up, perhaps egg cups or spools. Colored patches also work well. Ensure these objects are as scent-free as possible by washing them with soap and hot water and rinsing them well with fresh water.

Variety and Working off Leash

Above all, remember that tracking and searching should never become fixed patterns of work. Variety keeps it interesting for your dog. If he always has to sort the same old batons in the same old field, your dog will not have fun. In addition, remember that although we recommend a particular methodology, every dog has his own characteristics that must be taken in account during training.

It is also important that you never put your dog on a leash during the sent-identification line-up exercise. If you use the leash, you are not giving your dog the freedom he needs to work independently; you also may inadvertently warn your on-leash dog by slowing your pace or stopping when he arrives at the correct object, and this is a mistake you don't want to make. Your dog must be the one to find and point and retrieve, not you.

Don't fall into a fixed pattern when you train your dog to work with scent-identification line-ups. If you vary the work, it remains interesting for your dog. If he always has to sort the same objects in the same field with the same scents, his performance will suffer.

Three Parts

The previous exercise has no other purpose except getting your dog used to systematically working in a straight line over a line-up of objects, each of which must be smelled. Only when your dog does this correctly, and not before, can you practice actual scent identification. The difficulties associated with scent identification must each be overcome one by one; therefore, we have divided our training method into three consecutive parts:

Part 1: Sorting the Odor of the Handler
Part 2: Sorting the Odor of a Person Known and Sympathetic to the Dog
Part 3: Sorting the Odor of People Totally Unknown to the Dog

FIVE EXERCISES

For each of these parts, we have compiled five consecutive exercises. These exercises match in all the three parts.

The five exercises for Part 1 have the dog picking out the handler-odor-laden object from a choice of several objects with:

1. A "neutral" scent,
2. "The same weak" scent,
3. "The same strong" scent,
4. "Various weak" scents, and
5. "Various strong" scents.

For Part 2, we do the same five exercises, except in this case the dog must pick out the object with the scent of a well-known and sympathetic person. Finally, for Part 3, the same five exercises are also practiced; in this case the dog must identify the object with the scent of the unknown person.

Part 1: Sorting the Odor of the Handler

The five exercises noted above require detailed explanations, and so below we describe how to practice them associated with Part 1. Exercise 1 is already described in the previous section of this chapter.

To perform Exercise 2, ask someone who rarely or never comes in contact with your dog to keep a dozen of the well-known wooden batons in his or her trouser pocket for at least half an hour. After that amount of time, the batons will hold a strong odor of that person. Ask your scent supplier to place the batons in a clean, metal container and to close it up before giving it to you.

When these batons are exposed to fresh air for a while, they will lose their strong odor. So, using your tongs or pliers, take the batons out of the tin and place them in a cool spot, if possible hung up in a clean rope or wire net. Let the batons air out for about 24 hours, after which they, according to our experience, will still bear some "weak" scent. Put them back into the tin container with the tongs and take it to the training site. In the meantime, make sure you have your leather wallet and about six other wooden batons in your pocket, keeping them in there for at least half an hour.

We have already extensively described what has to happen next. Make the line-up by placing one of your pocketed batons in the first position, and the weakly scented batons in positions two to six. Give your dog the scent of your wallet and make sure, once again, that he can find your scented object in all places in the line-up.

The transition from Exercise 2 to 3 is gradual. The batons of the scent suppliers are gradually exposed less and less to the fresh air, and eventually you practice with them "fresh" from the hands of the scent supplier.

Exercise 4 differs from the foregoing exercise only in that each baton has a different odor. When you make the line-up of six objects—fewer than this is definitely not recommended—five people have to supply you with their odor. This could cause some problems because all the scented batons should remain strictly separated, and yet they must also be transportable. In the old days, all kinds of ingenious "sorting boxes" were designed, but with the current possibilities of "odorless" cans and drums—or, better, glass containers—you can place the individually packaged batons into another box, and the problem is overcome.

Exercises 4 and 5 flow gradually into each other, and finally the baton scented by you, the handler, can be found and retrieved amongst five other batons bearing strange and "strong" odors.

Part 2: Sorting the Odor of a Person Known and Sympathetic to the Dog

The gap between Part 1 (Sorting the Odor of the Handler) and Part 3 (Sorting the Odor of People Totally Unknown to the Dog) requires a set of transition exercises to help the dog move from "odor of the handler" to "odor of strangers."

Dogs unconsciously connect certain memories to certain odors.

Assume that your dog, albeit unconsciously, ties memories to different types of scents that may help him as he sorts out the line-ups. Indeed, as sighted humans recognize people through vision, the dog recognizes things through his nose. It is probably correct to say that if the dog sorts or follows a track, he has a grip on the scent he must follow not only because he was given the scent by his handler but also because he has a memory of that scent, or something similar to it. The odor in question is perhaps familiar to him and therefore he is more likely to absorb and remember that odor. In any case, we find that Part 2, Sorting the Odor of a Person Known and Sympathetic to the Dog, is an absolutely necessary step in training to ensure a good performance.

We deliberately ensure that the scent is from a person "known and sympathetic" to the dog. After all, dogs have memories of people with whom they come in contact in a less than pleasant way. Several times we have encountered dogs that would not fetch the objects that smelled like a particular person. They smelled the batons scented by the person and then showed us very clearly that they disapproved of the odor. They would only retrieve those objects when forced.

Since training with coercion in any form is out of the question, in this part, you should only ask someone well known and loved by your dog to be the scent supplier. In this part, as with Part 1, the exercises flow out step by step, from Exercise 1 to 5. The first time you take objects from people in your dog's immediate environment, and then you gradually expand the circle.

If your dog does not want to work seriously, bring the scent supplier to the working site and ask him or her to play with your dog for a while in a friendly manner.

Note that in addition to supplying scent to the batons, the scent supplier must also transfer his or her odor to a wallet or glove, which you can give your dog at the beginning of each exercise so he knows what scent he needs to find. All of the supplier-scented objects must be transported to the training site in the same container that carries the correspondingly scented batons.

Make sure your dog always finds the odor that matches the scent you give him before he sets out to examine the line-up.

The five exercises of Part 2 should be trained in the same serious manner as Part 1 because minutiae often make the difference in terms of success or failure. Success in training scent-identification line-ups often depends on a high degree to attention to details, as well as on gradual, step-by-step training.

BLIND SORT

Once your dog is properly working out this series of five exercises, you can introduce another exercise, the so-called Blind Sort. This exercise cannot be missed in practice—and it is also an essential exercise as a control. During the Blind Sort, your dog gets the scent, scans the line-up, but should not be able to find an object with a corresponding odor.

Training this part requires some caution, because it strongly deviates from the ordinary rule. After you command, "Fetch," your dog will do his utmost to bring you an object. If he reaches the end of the line-up without finding anything, he will easily be tempted to turn around in the firm belief that he has made a mistake and will therefore displease you, his handler.

In this special case we deviate from the rule not to speak during sorting. To help your dog when he reaches the end of the line-up without finding the appropriate object, kindly call him back to you and let him be sure that you are satisfied with his achievement. Always take care to sufficiently vary and repeat this exercise, without overdoing it.

There is another snag to this exercise. Make sure you do not vary your behavior when giving your dog the scent during the Blind Sort. Don't help your dog by nonchalantly giving him the scent, even though you know nothing is out there for him to bring back. You dog will notice the change in your attitude. To avoid this, you may wish to work with a reliable helper who makes the line-up and doesn't tell you when he or she is putting together a Blind Sort until the end, when the dog comes up with nothing to retrieve.

When asking your dog to sort "blind," give him a scent that does not match up with any of the scents in the line-up. Make sure you do not do this casually or nonchalantly—give him the scent as thoroughly as you would if there were a matching scent in the line-up. Otherwise, your dog will notice your change in behavior.

Part 3: Sorting the Odor of People Totally Unknown to the Dog

After you and your dog have properly worked through Parts 1 and 2, you will arrive at the last series of five exercises, where you ask your dog to examine and sort entirely foreign odors. However, remember that even if you take every step carefully, a major difficulty always remains. You see, it is a difficult task to ask your dog to remember a totally unknown odor. The expectation in this third series of exercises is that your dog can take the scent once and remember it until he discovers an object replete with the same odor.

So, when working on the exercises in Part 3, make sure you take time and pay attention while giving your dog the scent. Your dog may sometimes show hesitation, and if you notice that, immediately go back to the previous exercise and give your dog more time to sniff the air around the wallet or glove. Remember: never help your dog, because then the previous exercises will lose their value.

Throughout these more difficult exercises, bear in mind that you will make a disaster of all your training if you introduce punishment. Never forget that it is impossible to force your dog to use his nose. If your dog clearly indicates that he is not in the mood for the task, he cannot be stimulated by punishment to work. The only thing that helps in this case is your own creativity and powers of deduction. Try to root out the reason why your dog is failing in his attempts to perform the exercise, or why he isn't interested in performing. Remember that your dog may not be feeling well. A dry nose is a common phenomenon. As well, if his internal mucous membranes are dry, it is almost impossible for him to smell. If this is the case, break off practicing temporarily and contact a vet.

As we've already stated, we're presenting our method here in a general way, and you must always take into account the nature of your own dog. For example, one dog may require a good look in the eye, and perhaps a few unkind words, in order that he come back around to working. Another dog may need caresses on his head and shoulders, and to be told several times explicitly what a "Good boy" he is. Another may need to be lured into a romp. Know your dog's character so you will know what he needs when he's in a rut.

Remember that if you move too quickly through the steps as you train your dog, you will increase your dog's chances of failure. Your dog will certainly find it detrimental if, in short succession, he jumps from sorting your odor in the baton line-up to a bunch of different, foreign odors. Especially during the beginning of each part of scent-identification training, only work on one odor a day. Also, remember that even dogs that appear to have extraordinary talent must wait at least a few hours before receiving the scent of another unknown odor. In other words, don't inundate your dog with too many odors at once. Only at the last stage of training can you expect your dog to sort different odors, one after the other; make sure you don't start too early with that training. And, as with everything in our method, slowly and gradually reduce the time you give your dog between sorting two different odors.

Once you have thoroughly given your dog a new, unknown odor to sort, he will not easily forget it. However, because it is impossible for a dog to work rationally, he will sometimes involuntarily make mistakes. Remember, too, that how big the difference in odor is between different people is an open question. In our opinion, the best way to think about your dog's difficulties with the odor sort is to think about a large number of colored patches that only have minor differences. For example, take six shades of red. If you intensively examine one of the color patches, giving it your full attention, and then go to a line-up of the other patches, you will definitely realize how easy it might be to choose the wrong color. If you were successful in this color test the first time, you nevertheless will find out that after some repetitions, errors will come into play. Thus, to reduce your dog's chance of making mistakes, when you begin training Part 3, give him sufficient opportunity to "forget" a once-perceived odor before introducing him to a new one.

The Practice

When you have finished training Part 3, your dog has theoretically finished the sort training. But to be used as a service dog in everyday practice, you and your dog must undergo extra training. Some of the exercises we recommend may also be interesting for non-service dogs.

Until now you have only let your dog sort out of similar objects because you were making it clear to him that he should only pay attention to differences in odor, rather than to differences in form. In addition, until now you have only worked with wooden objects because, for various reasons, these are most practical.

TRAINING SCENT-IDENTIFICATION DOGS

Sorting odors in glass jars held up on metal stands.

Found!

It is now necessary to use objects made out of other materials: iron, stone, porcelain, glass, plastic, and rubber, among others. As well, use disparate objects, such as a line-up of the following items: pocket knife, wallet, key, screwdriver, flashlight, pliers, and gloves. At this stage it is also necessary to use objects that your dog doesn't retrieve often in training but objects that present themselves in real-life situations: clogs and other footwear, headwear, handkerchiefs, and so on. Also practice the scent-identification line-up in different places: indoors and outdoors, in corridors, attics, and barns, or any other place you can imagine.

Another thing service dogs need to practice is sorting "cold" (weak) scents. In real-life situations, it usually takes a long time before a dog is called in to begin a scent identification. The found objects that the dog must sort have long been out of touch with a human body and are thus equipped only with a cold scent. This kind of scent is in contrast to the "warm" (strong) smell of an object that has just been touched.

When you started training your dog to sort objects by scent, the "correct" batons were equipped with a stronger odor than the other objects in the line-up. Later these batons bore at least the same strength of odor as the others.

As a rule, however, in practice, a cold object is placed between warm ones. So, you must seriously train your dog to sort cold scents. Expose the objects to be sorted to fresh air for some time, and gradually make this amount of time longer and longer. As well, remember that in practice, the cold objects may be touched by someone else before being part of a line-up, so ask someone to gently touch the cold objects you are using in your training exercises.

Your service dog must also become accustomed to receiving the scent in different positions. It is not always possible to give your dog the scent while he is lying down. Perhaps the object cannot be laid on the floor, or perhaps the dog cannot lie down. Service dogs should be used to sitting and standing to receive the scent. If you can pick the object up with tongs or pliers, do so and hold it some distance from your dog's nose before giving the command "Smell." By his own initiative, your dog should approach the object and, sitting or standing, smell it. Some objects, however, cannot be picked up. In such cases, you can only point to the object, if necessary with your tongs, and then give the command "Smell." Objects that cannot be picked up might include seats (benches, chairs, seats of cars and bicycles); footprints in the soil, on windowsills or window frames; and places where a person's hands have been (doorknobs, switches, window panes). Train your dog with a variety of these objects because the more variety there is in training, the better he will understand the intention of this command in practice, which in turn can be decisive for the success of the job.

Finally, we would like to emphasize that real-life practice always surprises, and it is impossible to train for everything in advance. When you and your dog come across a surprise in the field, it's your job to try to reduce the situation to a learned exercise. To be successful, it is absolutely necessary that you have full confidence in your dog, which is only possible if from the beginning you have trained him to work independently and quietly after your initial command.

Another responsibility you have to your dog in practice is to honestly consider every situation you are called to. Ask yourself if there is a reasonable chance for success. If not, it is better to inform the authorities at the site (who expect much of the scent-identification or tracking dog) that there is no chance for success and that you and your dog will not investigate. We know from experience that this is not an easy thing to say, but it can be the right thing to do for your dog and for the case that is being investigated.

8

Training Tracking Dogs

By nature, every dog tracks for his own purposes. But we want to have tracking dogs that are useful to us. So, we have to teach dogs the special requirements for tracking. What do we require of tracking dogs in practice? A good tracking dog needs to be cool, calm, and persistent in order to work out a human track. He must do the work all by himself because in real life there is no one who can help him.

Tracking dogs must also be able to sort, both objects and people, coolly, calmly, and independently. In practice, it is simply impossible for human handlers to verify that their dogs are following a track, let alone the correct one. Sure, every now and then the dog lifts a corner of the veil when he gives a positive indication of the track in the form of a found object, a seemingly correct footprint, or something like that. But in between finding things, it is impossible to know if he is on the right track.

As the handler, you must simply follow your dog, step by step, however strangely he may be moving around: staring intently at the track, nose on the ground, then in the air, then back on the ground again. It is absolutely necessary for you to have full confidence in your dog. Unfortunately, in practice we have seen some dog handlers who seem to want to demonstrate their superior

The human track through morning dew is only visible to us for a short time, but a dog can smell it for much longer.

sense of smell, given the many corrections and instructions that they give to their dogs.

Requirements for a Tracking Dog

Really good tracking work is possible when you, the handler, have complete confidence in your dog. Of greater importance, perhaps, is that your dog has confidence in himself; he must, after all, work out the track alone. So, the first requirement for a tracking dog is that he have great confidence and be able to stand on his own four feet. In addition, he must be able to delve into the track and the tracking work and not be distracted by every little thing.

No one can coerce a dog to track. It is certainly possible to make a dog walk with his head down, just as it is possible to force a dog to retrieve an object he encounters. But to follow a track, working enthusiastically with his nose—no one can make a dog do that. And yet compulsion comes into practice sometimes because there are those who do not believe that dogs, purely for their own

No one can force a dog to track, especially in difficult situations such as this paved road.

pleasure, will slowly, step by step, follow a track. We're not talking about hunting dogs and their work here; that work is quite different and includes factors that play completely different roles for the dogs in question.

The most important features that we like to see in a working dog—in the broadest sense of the term—are the same ones that we need for a tracking dog: independence, courage, boldness, and fearlessness. But there is more. Although you cannot force a dog to track using outright coercion, you can force a dog to track without using coercion. Maybe this sounds impossible, but it isn't.

Obedience is the main requirement for all working dogs, and so it is for the tracking dog. At all times, even the hardest, the dog must do what he is told. The working dog slowly gets used to obeying. Obedience is not taught through a few exercises—it must be systematically cultivated. By making the conditions under which the dog has to work progressively more difficult, he will finally obey under all circumstances. The "habit" to obey will thus become second nature to a well-trained working dog.

Take, for example, the protection dog. Proper training involves gradually teaching obedience. In international examination regulations, as we've discussed in our book *K9 Schutzhund Training*, there are several exercises that lay a good foundation for obedience, provided that you, the handler, teach these exercises in the proper sequence. The same exercises are useful in teaching your tracking dog. Those who wish to have tracking dogs that can work in practice should start with the firm intention of training their dogs as police or protection dogs. If it turns out that your dog's character makes such training impossible, then at least you will also know that your dog will not be a good tracking dog, either.

Working-dog training is essential to acclimate your dog to perform quiet, thoughtful work, and to follow all given commands. Only the dog that is accustomed to obeying and that can work independently stands a chance at being a good tracking dog.

Only the dog that is accustomed to obeying and that can work independently stands a chance of being a good tracking dog.

Requirements for a Tracking Dog Handler

It is also important to know what you need to know and do to be a good tracking dog handler. You, the handler, must know your goal and should be fully aware of the nature and difficulty of tracking work. So, what is tracking? It is the perception of, searching for, and acceptance of a certain odor.

When people train their tracking dogs, they almost always start with a short track. As a rule in this training, we have seen that handlers lay out a track that is 33 to 66 feet (10–20 m) long through the grass, preferably using a slow and dragging gait. Then, they point at the visible track and push their dogs' heads down, making the poor animals "follow" this track. This, however, is not the way to train a tracking dog, as we will soon make clear.

A dog trained in this fashion does not use his nose; the problem is that the track is clearly visible and the dog can follow it with his eyes. Moreover, starting tracking training with an exercise that is not the easiest to learn, and cannot be controlled, gives dogs a distorted picture of what they must learn. Any track, wherever it might be placed, is a complex thing that is too difficult for a novice dog to work out.

While tracking the handler should watch the behavior of the tracking dog.

Complex Odor

If you lay a track in a meadow overgrown with grass and low plants, the composition of that human track is as follows:

1. The incredible variety of odors of crushed vegetation.
2. The odor of the earth that has been released with every footstep.
3. The odor of animals that live in and on the ground, as well as their droppings.
4. The track-layer's scent, which is hopefully not competing with the scent of other people and large animals.

The young, quite untrained dog, plunked down in front of the track described above, must somehow pick up the scent of the track-layer amidst this complex of odors. And who is to say that he does—even if it looks like he does. Because the track described above is invisible, he will be tempted to bring his nose down and smell the ground. But what delicious smell captures his nose? We cannot know because we do not have the noses required to check it out.

Begin with Sorting

Regardless of the difficulties associated with all tracks, there is a good method you can use to begin training your tracking dog. Our tracking training method is successful, and it begins with training the dog the scent-identification line-up, as described in the previous chapter.

Sorting is the basis for all search work. Tracking is, after all, nothing more than constant, consecutive sorting of different odors. When teaching your dog to sort, start by offering only a single scent that you can easily check. Moreover, when you teach him to sort, make sure he works independently. These are the conditions required for the foundation of tracking.

Introductory Exercises

Some people are talented at playing musical instruments without having had any training. Their ability comes from an innate talent. The music played by such people may be beautiful, but it will always be distinguished by a lack of technique, which highly trained musicians have learned and which allows them to receive accolades the world over for their combination of talent and training. The same is true with dogs: practically all dogs are innately talented sniffers. But only with training will they be able to achieve the highest accolades in tracking.

Learning the correct way to pick up the odor on a track forms the basis for further search work. Therefore, after teaching your dog to sort, you start out on a track by teaching your dog to pick up the scent at the start of the track. Make sure you allow your dog to take the time he needs, just as you do when giving him the scent during scent-identification exercises.

To give your dog the scent at the start of a track—so, the footprint—consider what you did when giving him the scent on objects: ask him to lie down just before the start and calmly say that familiar word: "Smell."

It is good if your dog's nose is resting about a quarter of the way into the start area (find steps for setting up the start area on page 134), so three quarters of it is in front of his nose. This way, your dog's nose is entirely surrounded by scent, and with every breath he takes—whether he likes it or not—he can smell the footprints, taking the information into his olfactory organ, and thus into his brain.

Training this way, you, the handler, have a certain assurance that your dog will perceive the odor of the track. You do not have the same certainty that your dog receives the odor of the track in a standing position because he does not have his nose low enough to the ground to properly take in the scent, especially if the track is positioned in an unfavorable wind, or if the odor of the track is cold.

Your dog should take between eight and 10 breaths to fully pick up the scent at the start of the track. If necessary, you can calmly lay your hand on your dog's head when you ask him to "Smell," but you should not apply this slight pressure longer than necessary. Never press your dog's head into the track because he will resist this. Never use pressure when asking your dog to pick up the scent. Instead, praise and reward him as you ask him to smell: "Smell, good boy, smell." Remember never to be coarse or rough with your search dog. If he resists somewhat, you can overcome his opposition with mild compulsion, quietly talking to him and repeating the command "Smell."

The Influence of the Wind

When you ask your dog to pick up the scent at the start of the track, you should pay attention to air currents because they can confuse your dog when he starts to work out the track. Dogs can only pick up the scent with certainty if there is a headwind or, if that is impossible, a crosswind. If your dog has to pick up the scent at the start in a crosswind, make sure you are not standing upwind, otherwise your dog will only pick up your odor. Note that if there

Dogs must get used to not being distracted by wind or other tracks.

is a tailwind, you cannot be as sure that your dog will pick up the scent well, especially if he is standing at the start with his nose four inches (10 cm) above the ground.

At the start you should also ensure that no people or other animals are in the immediate vicinity, much less standing "in the wind." The drifting scents of people and animals can confuse your dog as he starts to sort out the track.

Laying the Track

Often the beginning of the track—the start—is created in too exaggerated a fashion by the track-layer, who wipes his or her feet firmly on the ground, damaging plants and soil. This is bad enough, but usually the track-layer also goes on to lay the track by dragging his or her feet. This way of laying a track only causes problems for the novice dog when he tries to work out the track.

When you rub your shoes against the soil and plants, strong odors are released that mask the human odor on the track that you want the dog to pick up. Moreover, if your dog becomes used to the strong odor of damaged soil and plants, it is quite possible that he will begin to follow that smell more often than that of a track-layer.

Instead, it is best make the start and the track as is desired in many tracking exams: stand with your feet together at the beginning of the track, insert a stake into the ground on your left side, stay in that spot for about one or two minutes, and then lay the track by taking normal steps forward (not dragging your feet). By doing this, you leave more than enough human odor behind for your dog, even if he doesn't work out the track until hours later.

A big mistake handlers often make during tracking training is rapidly changing the odor source (the scent of the track-layer). So, perhaps the dog has to work out a track laid by the handler and shortly thereafter another track laid by another person. Searching and tracking require great mental effort from dogs, and handlers often underestimate the amount of work their dogs do as they work out a track.

Just like a scent-identification line-up, tracking is a physically and mentally intense exercise for dogs.

Just as a child must learn to read, a tracking dog must learn to read tracks. The child must learn the individual letters in a word before she can read it, let alone learn to read phrases, sentences, and paragraphs. Should you ask the child to read more words than she is capable of at the beginning, she will likely be frustrated and start to mix up the letters and words. Think about odors as the tracking dog's "words." Especially in the beginning of tracking training, the dog must be asked to follow a scent that he knows well; only after he has learned to follow this scent correctly can he be introduced to a different odor. And only when he is accustomed to that odor should he be asked to work with another scent. Always begin training your dog with your odor, the odor of the handler, and only after he has demonstrated success with this odor should you introduce a new one.

When training your dog to search and track, never follow one odor after another in quick succession, especially in the beginning. It is not exactly known how long an odor remains in the olfactory organ, or in the dog's brain, although we know that the odor is stored in his memory. The amount of lag time an odor occupies in the olfactory organ, and thus in the mind of your dog, will greatly depend on the impression that the odor or its conditions have made on him. To give a novice dog the opportunity to be successful, therefore, we must give him enough time to get rid of one odor before giving him a new scent with which to work.

Tracking Harness and Leash

Fit your dog with a tracking harness when training him to track. It will give him plenty of free movement and does not tighten up like a collar or chain around the neck. However, make sure you get your dog used to the harness before taking him out to a track. Put the harness on him at home or in the backyard, then fasten his usual leash to it and allow him to walk around for about 10 minutes, the leash dragging. Do this a few days in a row, and he will soon be used to wearing the harness.

Note that when a dog is seriously learning to track, he must work on a leash. He must become used to working on the leash; he must walk slowly so that you can follow him quietly and at a normal pace. If your dog pulls on the line and tries to run while tracking, you will have a hard time following him, and he will not learn to track properly.

Tracking on a long leash has the same purpose as heeling on leash in the obedience exercises. When you ask your dog to heel on leash, you ready him for off-leash heeling. When you teach your dog to track on leash and quietly walk the track, you ready him for the same behavior on the track without a leash.

When you begin tracking, attach the long line to the harness's ring, located on your dog's back. We don't recommend tracking with a collar and leash because the dog associates the leash with heeling. While tracking, the dog must walk ahead of you, the handler; while heeling, he must stay beside you. So, tracking with the collar and leash can present problems later with heeling.

And by the way, the idea that attaching the line to dog's collar will result in pulling the dog's head down and making him track with a deep nose, close to the ground, is nonsense. Only the dog's own interest in the track will encourage him to bring his nose down. If the dog has a good search drive, he also will be interested in a track.

You must habituate your dog to working with the harness and long line on the track. Do this on a track that is easy for him to follow: a straight track of about 164 feet (50 m), without turns, laid by you, the handler, at the end of which an object is placed. Immediately after laying the track, ask your dog to work it out. You must know exactly where the track is, so if your dog loses the track, you can gently guide him back to it. The best time to do this exercise is in the morning, when dew is still on the ground and you can easily see where you walked to make the track. You could also try this in snow.

In the beginning, the long line should be no longer than 13 to 16 feet (4–5 m). With a 33-foot (10-m) line, you simply cannot systematically train your dog to track. Some people say that when the handler is 33 feet away, he or she is less likely to disturb the dog, but this is nonsense. In the beginning, the dog likes to track with the support of his handler.

Speedy and Slow Searchers

Make sure you give your dog the scent in a prolonged way at the start of the track, and then let him search. At first, make sure the line extends out just behind the ring to which it is attached, but later on let it slide in your hand to the handgrip at the end of the line. This way you can respond to your dog if he wants to run over the track, tightening your hold on the line so he feels some resistance. In the beginning, hold him back slightly, but gradually hold him back more and more, so that after a few sessions, you are able to follow him at a normal pace.

However, note that you should not force your dog to only track at a slow pace. Dogs that are passionate for the track and have a good nose will not work at a leisurely pace—they will take no pleasure in tracking that way. On the other hand, dogs that move very slowly on a track may either have a bad nose but still a degree of search drive, or they may have physical problems with their sense of smell as a result of, for instance, medications such as antibiotics.

Praise your dog when he finds an object on the track.

Another reason for slow tracking may be that the dog doesn't have the drive to search and is being taught to track with force.

If your dog is searching the track too violently, slowly reel him in, without jerking on the line, to an almost stationary position. As you hold him back, slowly enunciate the word "Slow." Now, allow the leash to slowly slide in your hand, saying, almost singing, "Search, slow."

If your dog has been disturbed by your pulling on the line and becomes distracted—doesn't want to bring his nose back to the track—walk on slowly beside him to the next object on the track, with your hand in front of his nose all the while, pointing to the track on the ground and making sniffing noises yourself, motivating him to "Search." If your dog grabs the object, reward him exuberantly. Let him bring the object to you, carefully take it from him, and bring him back over to the spot on the track where he found it.

Problems

Even dogs with a sufficient search drive can lose that drive when being compelled to track on leash. If your dog is like this, don't lose your temper, but try to motivate him through fetch and search games, which should help him get his search drive back. After playing the games, go quietly back to the track to search for the objects. If your dog finds constant success on the track, consistently finding articles, and then is rewarded for his work, his search drive should flourish again.

If your dog is having significant trouble searching on leash, sometimes let him search without a leash, as you did when he was younger. Once your dog is accustomed to working on the line, you can gradually stop allowing him to search off of it. But never stop playing the retrieving and searching games because they represent rewards to your dog and are thus incredibly important.

Too often, handlers train their dogs to track incorrectly. As a result, these handlers have trouble with this part of their dog's training. Even though all dogs are fully capable of searching and tracking, we must still teach them to track in a systematic way for our purposes. Many dogs lack the proper foundation to perform the search work we want them to perform: they have enough drive to search or track, but they don't like the usual methods people use to train them. Therefore, our training method always begins with the challenge of increasing dogs' drive to search and track and their pleasure in those activities by playing all sorts of retrieving and searching games with them.

The first exercises related to tracking will have little connection to searching work in real life, just as many of a child's first lessons will not relate to the job she or he chooses later on. However, both the dog in training and the child at school receive an education delivered according to a method that provides them with a broad foundation that gives them a base for future learning.

It's a mistake to start training a dog to track before he knows how to sort odors. The source of many tracking errors is a lack of technical education: a dog trained without a clear methodology is given problems that are only possible for him to solve with a good technical foundation, resulting in errors. What does this foundation look like? To understand the types of techniques a dog needs in order to track successfully, you must first understand tracks and how they come into being. Then, you can determine the correct techniques required by tracking dogs and train those dogs using a systematic method.

Types of Tracks

The nature and course of different tracks include the following:

1. The pure foot track—this track goes over a terrain on which there are no other tracks.
2. The cross-track—this track surrounds tracks leading in the same or opposite direction or crosses another track.
3. The crossover track—this track goes over another, and therefore older, track.
4. The cross-under track—this track is covered by another, and therefore younger, track.
5. The interrupted track—this track goes through water (ditch, stream, canal); it is interrupted by the water and continues on the other side.
6. The broken-off track—this track stops suddenly, for example because the track-layer got into a vehicle, such as a boat or car.
7. The animal track—this is a track made by cattle, wildlife, birds, cats, or other dogs.
8. The track with a start—this track begins right after the place where a dog can first smell the odor of the track (the start).
9. The track without a start—this track has no clear place where the dog can be given the scent. When the beginning of the track is unknown, the dog will have to search for the track's entirety.

10. The warm track—this track is not older than half an hour.
11. The semi-warm track—this track is not older than one or one and a half hours.
12. The cold track—this track is more than two hours old.
13. The track on favorable ground—this track's surface is favorable because it retains odor well and keeps it smellable for a long time; an example is a soft track such as a field, pasture, or forest.
14. The track on less-favorable ground—this track's surface soil is hard but still porous, so it can still absorb odors (cobbled roads, cart tracks, footpaths, wooden surfaces).
15. The track on unfavorable ground—this track exists on any paved surface, such as smooth stones or tiles, or new asphalt.

The Influence of Weather

Weather plays an important role in tracking. When you are out tracking with your dog, consider the heat or cold, dryness or moisture of the soil and the air, as well as rain, snow, and wind. The weather can favorably or unfavorably influence the dissolution of the odor on the track. Heat, for example, does not have such a negative impact on the track as is generally assumed. However, for the dog, hot weather is not easy to work in. Cold weather is—completely contrary to the truth—also said to be detrimental to the track.

Much worse than heat or cold is drought, by which the soil is hardened and therefore less able to retain scents. Moist soil and damp air, however, have a beneficial effect on a track. Rain, especially persistent rain, however, can wash a track away. However, after a brief rainstorm, an old track can emerge as a stronger odor. The odor of a track under a thin layer of snow is clearly perceptible for your dog. Tracks in snow are generally easy for dogs to work out.

Strong winds can blow the odor of a track away (the windblown track). The odor is blown into the air and dilutes. Wind can also stir up the odors in a track between trenches and other irregularities in the soil. It can also pick up odor particles and deposit them in ditches, crevices, ledges, or other uneven places on the terrain, and the odor can become trapped there for a longer time than if it had stayed on the track, easily perceptible for a dog. Such windblown odor particles are often deposited beside the track and have no direct connection to the track. A dog that is tempted by such windblown parcels of odor can easily lose the original track.

Knowing these main terms and conditions of tracks, we have worked out a systematic way in which to train dogs to track.

The Tracking Exercises

In our method, tracking training consists of the following groups of exercises:

1. *Exercises on Warm Tracks* These include quiet walking during tracking; keeping to the track (the dog must not react to windblown odor); careful searching for a lost track (at turns); tracking through or over obstacles; and following longer tracks. These exercises all take place on a warm track.

The following exercises help your dog build up the subtleties of tracking form.

2. *Cross-Tracks*
3. *The Track on Different Types of Soil*
4. *The Track in Different Weather Conditions*
5. *(Much) Older Tracks*
6. *Animal Tracks*
7. *The Interrupted Track*
8. *Searching for a Track*
9. *Searching Back for Lost Objects*

Watching the Dog

Some say that the handler must always know exactly how the track is laid out. This statement is based on the false premise that humans can track better than dogs. As a result, some handlers use the strangest aids and tools while tracking with their dogs: thin posts, stones, and colored cloths; and in the forests, chalk marks on trees or colored threads and cloths tied on branches. All of this, however, distracts both the handler and the tracking dog, leading them away from what really matters: the intense track of the footsteps. Unfortunately, handlers who buy into this philosophy will only end up disturbing their dogs.

All the while, it really is so simple. Through his body and attitude, your dog shows you whether or not he is on the track. If you taught your dog to sort odors properly, and during the sorting paid attention to your dog's posture and expressions, then you know how your dog demonstrates he is on the right track.

All you need to do is carefully observe your dog's posture and expression as he tracks. His body language will tell you if he is on track. Watch him while he is at work and you will understand what his gestures and attitude mean in practice.

It bears repeating: do not try to know better than your dog, and do not disturb him in his work. During the sorting exercises, he learned to work independently, and that ability will come in handy now, on the track. For many handlers it is not easy to let their dogs do their own job. How often have you thought, "Oh, he should be turning left, not right," and slightly pulled him in that direction, only to find out later that your dog was right all along.

1. EXERCISES ON WARM TRACKS

In this series of exercises, you have to train your dog to perform the following parts:
- Slowly walking on the track;
- Keeping to the track in a crosswind;

- Waiting on the track (necessary when negotiating obstacles over which or through which a track can go); and
- Following longer tracks.

First, you, the handler, must lay out a U track. For our purposes here, we will assume the wind directions are as follows. The first part of the track runs against the wind (a headwind); after the first turn there is a crosswind from the left, and after the second turn there is a tailwind. Each straight leg of the track is about 262 feet (80 m) long, so the total track is 787 feet (240 m) long.

Your dog should have his tracking harness and leash on. At the start, give your dog the scent of the footprint by having him lie down and saying "Smell." Once he has taken in the scent, calmly command, "Search," and possibly even point with a finger to the track on the ground.

Since the first straight leg of the track goes against the wind, the smell of the track should easily reach your dog's nose, and your dog may wish to start out quickly. Stand in your place and let the line slip through your hands. The faster your dog sets out, the tighter you will want to hold the line, encouraging him to slow down. When the end of the line is in your hand, follow your dog. You may set out a bit quickly, but do not trot behind your dog; gradually reduce your speed to a normal pace.

If your dog is disturbed and stops, encourage him to track with a calm and friendly "Search." Move closer to him and hold the line shorter. When he regains the track, you can reward him—"That's a good boy"—and let the line slide through your hand again.

Now you must focus your attention on the first turn in the track. When your dog walks over and past the turn, after a few feet his body language will change. He will become restless, moving his head back and forth to search, and sometimes he will walk around in circles. This is a sign that your dog knows he has lost the track.

When you see this happening, stand still and let your dog quietly search on. Under no circumstances should you help him, except to encourage him with "Search" if he is not searching. Do not bother him. Your dog may walk until the end of the line, and if he wants to continue on, quietly say, "No," and motivate him again with "Search." You can point in a large arc to the track, which you know goes on to the right. Soon, your dog will find it and you will know by his change in body language that he is following it again. Say, "Good boy, that's the search."

If necessary, you may have to reduce your dog's speed again, but don't suppress his love of the search too much, too soon. Try to bring him back to a normal pace after about 66 feet (20 m).

This second leg of the track is buffeted by a crosswind from the left. Depending on the wind speed, your dog may drift away from the track a bit, but that's usually not a problem. If he later works on much older tracks, he will naturally remain closer to the main track.

Some handlers want to keep their dogs exactly on the track in crosswinds. However, this is a dangerous practice because then the dogs' independent work is interrupted. It is not a problem at this stage of training if your dog follows along about a foot and a half (0.5 m) off of the main track, tracking along the windblown track.

Work out the second turn in the same way you worked out the first one. If your dog doesn't walk over the turn but directly tracks right into the third leg of the track, praise him immediately.

About 98 feet (30 m) before the end of the track, let your dog wait. Slow your tempo, and via the taut line and the command "Wait," your dog will stop. Say, "Wait," again and walk calmly over to your dog. Now, command him to "Search" and point to the track. Praise him when he begins tracking again. If he doesn't continue searching, help him by walking beside him, sniffing loudly, and pointing at the track until you reach the object at the end of the track. Now, your dog can have fun playing with the object.

All of the influences you exert over your dog—making your dog walk slowly and wait—during this exercise may be more disturbing for some dogs than others. Assess for yourself how far you should go with your dog.

Once your dog gets accustomed to the various influences on shorter tracks, gradually make the tracks longer. Don't worry: if your dog can work out a 984-foot (300-m) track well, a track that is 1,640 feet (500 m) or longer will be no problem for him. Also, ask your dog to wait on the track for longer and longer periods, up to about one minute.

Generally speaking, after a dog has worked out his handler's tracks well a few times, he may be able to try working out a warm track laid by another person, preferably someone your dog knows well and loves.

2. CROSS-TRACKS

While he is learning to track, your dog must learn that as he works out a track (the main track) he should not be distracted by cross-tracks, which can be older or younger, parallel, or crossover or cross-under tracks. Your dog will have some basic training in this from his sorting exercises, but he has to be absolutely sure at sorting before you start training him to handle cross-tracks.

For the cross-track exercises, we need one or more helpers as track-layers, and it is good to mark the points where the cross-tracks are, preferably using natural markers such as trees, fences, or bushes. As your dog works out the track, ask the track-layers to let you know if the dog is following the main track correctly.

Begin the exercises on a warm, helper-laid track that is between 328 and 492 feet (100 and 150 m) long. The first search tracks you ask your dog to work out should be straight, and no parallel track should exist beside the first 164 feet (50 m) of that main track. After that distance, however, a second helper should lay a parallel track beside the main track, extending it all the way to the end of the main track. In the beginning, only work with a headwind or a tailwind, and make sure that the parallel track is just as old as the main track. The parallel tracks can be on the left or the right of the main track; regularly change up the track-layers for these tracks.

If your dog goes over to investigate the parallel track, give him some time to see if he comes back to the main one on his own. Perhaps he is merely curious about the second odor. Refrain from influencing him when he is on the parallel track; definitely do not speak any discouraging words. When he comes back to the main track, do reward him with the words "Good boy."

However, if he follows the parallel track farther on, apply a short jerk to the line and say, "No, search the track." If necessary, point to the main track and, if he comes back, praise him at once. Dogs that have learned to sort correctly will instantly realize what is required of them.

The next step is to lay main tracks that have turns, so that the turns are buffeted by crosswinds. Where the legs of the main track are in a crosswind, the parallel track should be about 6.5 feet (2 m) away from the main track and heading in the direction from which the wind is blowing. This way, the wind first hits the parallel track, so the dog will be able to smell it even as he works out the main track. You can also ensure that part of the main track does not have the parallel track, and that parallel track only comes in again after 33 to 66 feet (10–20 m). When you do this, you can easily determine if your dog is showing interest in the parallel track. Handle his interest in the parallel track as suggested above.

To further train your dog to be a stable tracker, add a parallel track to the part of the main track that has a crosswind, after the main track has extended about 164 feet (50 m) from the start. This parallel track should be about 1.5 feet (0.5 m) away from the main track, and it should keep going straight ahead when the main track makes a turn. Because the main track parts ways with the parallel track, you can easily determine if your dog is tracking on the right course.

The next step is to create a main track that has parallel tracks on both sides. Train this track the same way you trained the single parallel track.

Yet another variation is to create a main track that has a cross-track coming in from the side, entering the main track, and then going away from the main track. At another point, this cross-track can cross the main track again, but this time have it continue alongside the main track for 66 feet (20 m), or so, before crossing the main track again and going away. The angles at which this cross-track crosses the main track should be 90° at first. Later, you can include both obtuse and acute angles for the intersections. The risk of your dog going over to the cross-track increases with such angles.

After your dog is able to work out a series of main tracks that have cross-tracks interfering with them, begin laying a main track over top of other tracks. Only lay the main track over parts of an under-track, though. Remember that you should pay close attention to your dog when he is working out these more complex tracks, especially in the places where the main track leaves the under-track.

The next variation in training is to have your dog work out a main track with a cross-track on top. For this exercise, at first—as for the exercise above in which the cross-tracks are underneath—the parts where the main track is under another track should not be long. To properly train this exercise, make sure you have many track-layers helping you. Be careful: a person who lays a main track should only be able to lay a cross-track after about a week's break.

3. THE TRACK ON DIFFERENT TYPES OF SOIL

The first exercises of this type are on your own warm tracks. The transition from a favorable to a less favorable, and finally to an unfavorable soil must be made gradually. Pay attention; do not progress if your dog is having trouble on a certain type of soil. Stay on that surface until your dog overcomes his problems. Only then should you move on to lay a track on a more difficult type of soil.

The transition from a favorable to a less favorable, and finally to an unfavorable tracking terrain must be made gradually.

If your dog has many problems following the track on a certain type of soil, do not constantly practice on this surface. Instead, have the track start on an easier type of soil, move along the difficult soil for a while (at first for a short while, then longer and longer), and finally end on an easier type of soil.

If your dog is able to follow your track over the most difficult of surfaces, try training him on the warm tracks of different tracklayers, and later add cross-tracks—all on difficult terrain.

4. THE TRACK IN DIFFERENT WEATHER CONDITIONS

Most of the time, you must train in whatever weather presents itself. Never train only in good or favorable weather. This way, you can find out the types of weather in which your dog performs best.

Remember never to give your dog tasks in bad weather that he could not easily do in fine weather.

5. (MUCH) OLDER TRACKS

Start out by training these exercises on a track that you, the handler, make on a favorable type of soil. The length of the track is initially 984 to 1,312 feet (300–400 m); make the track shorter rather than longer. Lay three tracks, one after the other. Let your dog work out the first track 20 minutes after you make it. Pause

If you build up the tracking training in the right way, making it exciting and interesting for your dog, the working out of old tracks (even on unfavorable surfaces) will not be a problem.

at the end for about five minutes, then ask your dog to work out the next track. Pause again, and have him work out the third track.

If your dog has no problem with these tracks, the next time you lay the tracks, wait 30 minutes before asking him to work out the first track. Wait five minutes between tracks this time. By the time your dog gets to the third track, it will be much older than half an hour.

Continue to increase the age of the tracks. Have your dog work out the first track after 30 minutes, the second after 45 minutes, and the third after one hour. In this way, you increase the age of the tracks day by day, and soon you will see that your dog presents no problems with the older tracks.

The next step is to have other people lay these consecutive tracks. If your dog has trouble with tracks of a certain age, start again from scratch. Once he is successful with these stranger-laid tracks, ask your helpers to lay the same series of tracks on less-favorable soil. Ensure these tracks are short, at first, but if all goes well, increase their length.

PUSHING BOUNDARIES

If your dog should run into difficulty on a certain track laid by a stranger in this exercise, do not revert back to laying tracks yourself, but do consider the age of the track on which your dog is having the most trouble. At this point, continue to train your dog on a track laid by a stranger, but start with a track of an age that you know your dog can easily follow. The second track should be a little older, and the third track should be as old as the track on which you noticed your dog encountering difficulty. For example, your dog had trouble on a track laid on favorable soil that was three hours old. At that point, you stopped aging the tracks and started over again.

Start from scratch—but with a track laid by a stranger and not by you. So, for this example, you will have asked someone to lay three tracks, one to be worked out after two hours, the second after 2.5 hours, and the third after three hours. If the dog still has problems after this, then the age of each track should be decreased by a quarter of an hour, so the second after 2 hours 15 minutes, and the third after 2 hours 45 minutes.

Remember: never change the track-layer at the same time that you increase the age of the track. And only increase the age of the track by a quarter or half an hour every time.

6. ANIMAL TRACKS

It is not good for tracking dogs to follow game tracks (service dogs should not be hunting dogs), but we can perform interesting exercises with other animal tracks. Perhaps the most interesting one involves the track of a rider on horseback. When accompanying other animals, humans usually walk beside the animal or lead it—these tracks also provide interesting situations for your dog to work out. We can also make use of the tracks made by other dogs, which were led with a long line. Train your dog to work out these tracks in the same way he learned to search for human footsteps, except these exercises give your dog the scent of the animal that laid the track.

We doubt that such tracks are very useful for service dogs to learn, but all dogs appreciate the variety inherent in these exercises. The greatest enemy of tracking is, after all, the endless repetition of the same exercise on the same piece of land and the same surface.

THE END IS IN SIGHT

As you progress through these exercises on older tracks, bring cross-tracks into the picture. First add them as parallel tracks, then later have them cross the main track. Train your dog to work with such tracks on favorable ground, as well as on short stints of unfavorable ground, where he will be required to put in more effort.

You will eventually reach the point at which your dog's abilities do not allow him to progress any further. You will be surprised, however, at how far your dog can go. Depending on your efforts and motivation, and your dog's interest, his performance potential is great, and may seem almost impossible. For example, working out a track of human footprints that are eight to 12 hours old is no problem for a dog, big or small, purebred or mongrel. In the former Eastern Germany, tracking competitions used tracks that were 36 hours old.

See for yourself one morning how your dog nicely works out a track that was laid the previous afternoon. By building up tracking training the right way, and making it interesting for your dog, the working out of old tracks is no problem.

7. THE INTERRUPTED TRACK

Teach your dog to work out this kind of track near a shallow, narrow watercourse, such as a ditch or stream. The track-layer must remember the exact place where the track enters the water and where it comes out of the water. At first you can mark these spots with chalk on a tree or pole. For the first track, the track-layer should walk through the water for about 33 feet (10 m) and then continue the track on the bank opposite to where the track began.

When you and your dog arrive at the place where the track enters the water, your dog will not know what to do. Loosen the line and say, "Good boy, search." Stay on the shore and motivate your dog to go over the water. Remain on your side of the water, letting your dog search independently. If he goes too far, call him back quietly and point in the direction in which he can expect to find the track.

If your dog finds the track, praise him, but also immediately tell him to "Wait." He should wait while you cross the water and approach, taking the line again. Continue to praise him and encourage him to start tracking again—he will quickly find his reward, the object he can retrieve to you.

8. SEARCHING FOR A TRACK

In real-life practice, a track will not have a start, and it may happen that the track begins a few yards away from the place at which you give your dog the order to "Search." When you train this exercise, the track-layer should throw an object or piece of clothing belonging to him or her and walk away without making a start. The object should land a few yards to the side of where the track begins. The first tracks in this exercise are always made against the wind. Give your dog scent from the thrown object or clothing and then say, "Search the track."

Once your dog has found the track and continues along it, praise him, and then say, "Wait." At this point, put him on the line and say, "Good boy, search," so he is encouraged to keep going. Progress in this exercise by allowing him to search for the track from increasing distances.

9. SEARCHING BACK FOR LOST OBJECTS

In this exercise, your dog must retrace his steps to find an object you have dropped or lost. Only train this exercise when your dog is able to track quietly because a dog that has to go back to find something should be quiet.

Walk with your dog on leash without tracking on the tracking field—don't let him notice when you drop the object. About 164 feet (50 m) from where you dropped the object, point to the track you have made and say, "Search it." For this exercise, your dog must work the track out without a leash, all by himself.

This search back is gradually done from increasing distances. The next step is to let him search for objects dropped by other people who are walking with you. Later on, you and your dog will meet a stranger who has dropped an object on his track, which your dog must search. First, though, that person must walk with you for about 33 feet (10 m). For this version of the exercise, the stranger will give your dog the scent from his or her hands. In searching back, your dog must now leave your track and follow the track of the stranger. If necessary, you can accompany your dog to the place where you met the stranger, then encourage your dog to search the stranger's track from that point back. Remember that these exercises should only be attempted when your dog knows how to sort.

Tracking without a Line

Although we recommend that your dog begins by working out all tracking exercises on the line, you can start tracking without a line when your dog is able to calmly work out tracks. The transition from tracking on line to off can be done by letting go of the line so the dog drags it. The dog will still feel "bound," but he will also feel more independent without your influence.

A Dutch police officer and his dog work out a track after a bank robbery.

Only after tracking several times with a dragging line can you allow your dog to begin searching a track freely. Follow him from a distance and, if all goes well, increase that distance until he can work freely on longer tracks, too. If errors appear, or when you start in on a new group of exercises, use the line.

Searching Is Fun

We recommend training your dog to track freely to strengthen his independence and increase his stability as a tracker. In real-life practice, we always follow our dogs at a certain distance. Although the dog's work is reliable, we must be there to control it. Remember to continue to ask your dogs to perform sorting tests and play retrieving and search games throughout their lives. This is fun for both you and your dogs.

Training without a leash will build your dog's ability to work independently and increase his tracking skills.

9

Training Detector Dogs

Some members of the law-enforcement profession regard the detector or tracking dog as a useful extension of their power. Good dog handlers, however, modestly view themselves as the organizing extensions of their dogs, and they allow them as much freedom as possible when they are working.

I have seen delightful film footage showing a police detector dog endeavoring to draw his handler's attention to a cache of drugs that is nearby, but not precisely where the dog has just been directed to search. The handler is listening to another officer and steadfastly suppressing the dog's efforts until finally, the dog resigns himself, with a sigh, to the impenetrable stupidity of humankind.

This situation highlights the main shortcoming of the (detector) dog. Communicating with humans is difficult, and filing reports most of the time is impossible. If we could somehow know exactly what our dogs know, we could enormously increase our potential for scent detection.

Alert

Your dog will let you know if he has found a scent clue during a search by means of an alert, or response, consisting of a certain characteristic behavior. When you see your dog behave in this

DETECTOR DOGS WORKING ON LEASH: PROS AND CONS

Advantages: The dog is under better control, and he cannot wander away or be distracted. The leash motivates the dog and, through it, he feels connected to his handler. A leash can also help you, the handler, calm your restless or spirited dog down a bit. As well, a leash attached to your dog's collar or harness prevents your dog from running away when surprised. On the whole, when your dog is searching on leash, you are better able to steer and guide him.

Disadvantages: The leash can force the dog to conform to the expectations of the handler. The leash can also afford too much stress, performance pressure, and nervous tension. You may inadvertently pull your dog away from the correct spot. You, the handler, may become the searcher, not your dog. Nervous and impatient handlers can pull their dogs away from success and inspire insecurity in their dogs rather than confidence. Under pressure from his handler, the dog may become uncertain. Under the influence of the leash and his handler, the dog may become erratic and inaccurate.

---

way, you know he's found something. Each dog has a different way of communicating his find to his handler. In our training program, we insist that each handler and dog team have the room to develop their capacities and skills in their own individual way. There is no universal behavior that dogs adopt for an alert. You have to recognize for yourself how your unique dog indicates a place where something is to be found. If you give your dog the freedom to alert you in his own way, you allow your dog to develop and attain his goals.

It makes absolutely no sense to play retrieve games with dogs that don't like to retrieve. It also makes no sense to expect your dog to bark at a scent clue if your dog doesn't like to bark. Every dog has a natural tendency to let his handler—with whom he has a strong connection—know one way or the other that he has found something, or that he wants his handler to come with him to what he has

In our training program, it is fundamental that each handler and dog team have the room they need to develop their skills in a way that works for them.

found. To extend the principle to training, the handler—the person who can most accurately recognize his or her dog's alerts—should tell the instructor the location of a response. The searching dog has different ways of indicating during an operation or mission, depending on the time span and the degree of difficulty of the search action. During the search action, your responsibility as the handler to make decisions based on your dog's work is great. You don't want to yell out, "Here it is, force open," unless you are sure your dog has found what you are looking for. Any decision you make is a heavy burden, both in training and during an actual operation.

Behavior and Postures

A very important response a detector dog exhibits is his strong interest in a certain place, often accompanied by his refusal to leave it. Even if he walks away from the spot after exhibiting this behavior, he may only be going to get a breath of fresh air away from the area (or outside, if the search is taking place inside). After a short break, he will return to the spot and search it, for it has the highest odor concentration—and he will alert you to his find. It is very easy to tell when a detector dog has found something. He walks in a certain way, holds his body and ears in a certain way, and wags his tail in a certain way.

Don't ignore your dog when he is so interested in the odor of a certain spot that he won't leave it.

TRAINING WITH ONE OR MORE SCENTS?

Handlers consider what substances (such as drugs) their dogs will be working with when they choose scents for training. Some handlers choose to introduce their dogs to these scents one at a time. As soon as their dogs do well with the first odor, the handlers introduce the next one, together with the first one. It is possible to train your dog to recognize more than one scent at a time, which surely is a faster method. However, the step-by-step-method is more effective; when training your dog in this way, you can be sure he knows and recognizes each odor very well. The disadvantage to this method is that it takes more time to train than the second method.

Active Alerts

During training, the alert your dog gives you when he has found the odor he is trained to find is of great importance. Always choose to teach an alert that suits your dog's behavior and character. If your dog has a well-developed drive to find the odor he is trained for, you can rely on his alert.

Never forget to reward your dog for all his good work.

In detector dog training, there are both active and passive alerts. Active alerts consist of the following:

1. *Barking* The dog stays near the scent clue and barks repeatedly or continuously, so that the handler hears and can come to the dog. This type of alert is suitable for dogs that bark very easily on their own. Often this barking happens after scratching because the dog is irritated when he cannot penetrate the find. In some cases, barking by itself is not enough, and the dog has to indicate exactly where the highest odor concentration is coming from by scratching it or putting his nose in or toward it.

2. *Scratching* The dog scratches in an attempt to penetrate the covering to get to the spot with the highest concentration of odor. This type of scratching should not be confused with the so-called "orientational" scratching, by which the dog, to convince himself better of the odor, scratches away some covering with his forepaw. He does this to open, so to speak, odor canals in the material he is scratching.
3. *Biting* Mostly combined with scratching, we sometimes see the dog biting at whatever is covering up the highest concentration of odor to pull the covering away.
4. *Bringsel Alert* A dog trained in this method carries a small, soft (leather) baton, the bringsel, on his collar during a search. When he finds the scent clue, he picks up the bringsel by himself and brings it to his handler, who takes the bringsel and removes it from the collar. The handler asks, "Where?" or says, "Show me," and the dog leads his handler to the scent clue. There the dog has to pinpoint the exact location of the highest odor concentration by scratching or putting his nose to the scent clue. The bringsel alert works well for dogs that like to fetch. In addition to the dog bringing the bringsel to his handler, the dog also often displays remarkable excitement. He wants to make it clear to his handler that he has found something.
5. *Recall* The dog may try to entice his handler by walking to the found location and then back to the handler. He is usually very excited, and the walking to and fro between the find and the handler brings the handler to the scent clue.
6. *Physical Alert* The dog, with his physical attitude or a certain other behavior, makes it clear to his handler that he has found a scent clue. For example, he may come back to the handler, sit in front of him or nudge him.

Training an on-leash dog to find thrown weapons and exhibit an active alert.

A SAR dog exhibiting an active alert by barking and scratching.

TRAINING ACTIVE ALERTS

To train dogs to display active alerts, we let them learn by playing, then later on turn the behavior they have learned into a duty. For training we use a tennis ball with a small opening, a hollow block of wood, or a plastic or metal tube with small holes—the sides on all of these objects are firmly closed. We also use a roll-up constructed of several cotton fabric layers rolled together and secured by a rubber band or piece of cord.

First teach your dog to play fetch with the roll-up, ball, or tube. If he likes this game, place a well-packaged scent you want to train him on inside the fetch object. When he is retrieving the slightly odorous object well when you throw it right in front of him, start throwing it when and where your dog can't see it, and ask him to "Search." He will search for it but will not be able to find it right away. When he does find it, reward him with a treat or by playing fetch with another object, such as a ball. He will quickly get the idea that searching and retrieving will result in a reward, and he will easily learn to find the tube by its scent.

When he is doing well with this game, change the terrain, conditions, and other surroundings, and continue the game until your dog has a real passion for searching. By that time you should be using tubes made of different artificial materials (wood, iron, aluminum, leather, rubber), each containing its own scent. Do whatever you can to increase your dog's skill level and training. For example, slowly change up your practice terrain to places like train stations, post offices, barracks, cars, trains, buses, and so on, and practice with all kinds of scent-filled tubes in these new environments.

At first, you and your dog should play in the open air with one tube, ball, or roll-up; after that, do the same inside buildings, throwing the tube into various locations that are easy to find and accessible for your dog. Then, start training in other places with the other tubes or roll-ups. Depending on how you train—one odor after the other, or a few odors together—make sure you regularly change the odors as soon as your dog shows he can find them easily.

THE BARKING ALERT

Dogs can produce many different sounds, from deep, rolling barks to clear, high-pitched barks and cries. They use their voices to express themselves and can change the pitch and volume of their barks. It's not surprising, then, that many dogs can easily develop barking alerts.

For this kind of alert, your dog must know how to bark on command. First you must find something that gets your dog barking. You might need to be imaginative. For instance, try showing your dog his full food dish, holding it high enough that he can smell it but cannot reach it. His impatience may inspire him to bark. Other dogs can be brought to barking by sounds. When the barking prickle is found, with every bark you give a command such as "Bark," or "Loud." If he increases his barking, reward him: "Good boy, bark!" In the beginning, give him his reward after he barks two or three times; later on, let him bark a while longer before rewarding him. If your dog doesn't bark easily, don't repeat these exercises very often or he really won't want to bark.

Dogs that bark easily on their own may begin to bark at scent clues. The moment your dog starts barking at an indicated place, you should reward him. You may, however, need to help your dog in the beginning by giving the command "Bark" or "Loud" the moment he begins to smell the scent he is supposed to find.

Dogs may also bark to call their handlers over to where they have found something. We also often see detection dogs walk toward their handlers and make eye contact. Then they bark at the handlers and go back to the place where they found the scent. This sort of barking is often seen in dogs that are easily excited and are easy barkers. You see this behavior often in herding dog breeds, such as Australian shepherds and border collies. These dogs are not focused on the substance but rather on their handlers, keen to tell them about the find.

THE BRINGSEL ALERT

The bringsel alert is useful for dogs that like to retrieve but have trouble barking. During a search, such a dog carries a bringsel—a soft, leather baton—on his collar. When you start training this method, only use the bringsel in retrieving exercises. The dog that loves retrieving will enjoy picking it up and bringing it back to the handler. Be careful, though. The bringsel is not a toy and should be treated as a tool. Only use it during certain exercises, and don't let your dog play with it.

Before the beginning of each bringsel exercise, make sure your dog is wearing the leather collar on which the bringsel attaches, getting him used to wearing it as part of the search ritual. Lay the bringsel down close to the scent you want your dog to find. Send your dog over to the substance he needs to identify from a short distance (33 feet [10 m]); he'll find the bringsel there. Encourage him to pick it up and bring it back to you. As soon as you have the bringsel in hand, go with your dog back to the substance he found and reward him exuberantly with treats or play with a ball. To avoid confusing your dog, perform this exercise only once and then take a break. It is better to repeat the exercise after five or 10 minutes than it is to immediately begin another exercise.

If this exercise goes well, increase the distance to the scent clue, always making sure your dog is correct picking up the bringsel. The next step is to change the circumstances of the work, so hide the scent you want your dog to search for, together with the bringsel. Again, make sure your dog is able to find and pick up the bringsel near the place where you've hidden the scent. As soon as your dog knows the pattern of this bringsel alert, you can start decreasing the amount of help you give him. Your dog has found success in this exercise when he is able to search for the scent on your command, find the bringsel at the spot, and bring the bringsel back to you directly, without dropping it. He should then turn around automatically and run to the scent clue, where he should wait for his reward. Always accompany your dog back to the correct spot and, once there, praise him enthusiastically.

At this stage, you can attach the bringsel to your dog's collar, starting the exercise again, starting him off at a short distance (33 feet [10 m]) from the scented substance he needs to find. Send him to the scent, and use your voice to encourage him to pick up his bringsel. You may need a helper who can go to your dog and help him by placing his or her hand under the bringsel and lifting it high. Later on, your helper's light touch on the bringsel will be enough to motivate your dog to pick it up. If everything goes well, you can gradually increase the distance to the scent he needs to find, and add in more search work before he is able to find the scent clue. At this point you can also train your dog to search for other scents.

Some problems can crop up when training the bringsel alert. For instance, your dog may pick up the bringsel without finding the correct scent clue. If this happens, you should immediately correct him with "No," replace the bringsel, and then encourage him to continue on. Or, replace the bringsel and then restart the exercise. Additionally, try to make sure your dog isn't experiencing any strain or stress during the exercise (or even during an operation). When a dog is under pressure, he may try to please his handler (incorrectly) by picking up the bringsel, even if he hasn't found a scent clue.

Passive Alerts

Some dogs demonstrate passive alerts by sitting, standing, or lying down—no barking or scratching—near the scent clue. This passive response may be (but does not have to be) accompanied by the dog pointing his nose into the scent clue.

Wherever we go, we hear the same thing: "Passive-response dogs don't pinpoint, so how can you tell where the substance is with a passive dog?" However, if you have ever worked with properly trained passive-response detector dogs, you will know that they do pinpoint, and it is very easy to tell where the substance is.

We have experienced passive response in searches for drugs as well as when working with explosives detector dogs. In the beginning, we were a bit skeptical about passive response, but after a while we liked it and have trained dogs to use this method quite successfully. The advantages are obvious. There is less risk to the dog and handler when the dog exhibits a passive response instead of an active one, and there is no damage to private property.

After exhibiting a passive alert by standing next to the jacket, this drug-detector dog is rewarded with a ball.

TRAINING PASSIVE ALERTS

Begin passive-response training with a box that is about 12 inches wide, 12 inches long, 8 inches high (30 × 30 × 20 cm) and that holds the odor you want to train your dog to identify, as well as a tennis ball. On the top side of the box is an opening in which you can put the tennis ball. Train this exercise inside, in a room where there are no distractions.

Before starting, show your dog the ball and let him see you put it in the box so that he knows it's in there. Because your dog is crazy about his ball, he will go straight to the box to try to get the ball, sticking his nose right in the opening at the top. At that moment, give him the command "Sit." If he doesn't sit, command him again and quietly bring him into the Sit position, telling him he is a "Good boy."

Now point at the hole in the box, ensuring your dog stays sitting. The moment he puts his nose into the hole of the box and sits, enthusiastically praise him and, with your throwing hand behind the dog, throw a different ball for him to retrieve. Make sure your dog does not see you throwing that ball, or he will pay more attention to you than to the box he is supposed to be smelling. Each time he sticks his nose in the hole at the cover of the box to get his ball, your dog will smell the scent—or, in training with more than one odor at once, the scents.

After repeating this exercise many times over many training sessions, don't place the ball in the box but keep the scent or scents in there. Immediately after your dog sniffs, sits, and pinpoints the opening in the box, throw the ball for your dog and praise him for his good work. The next step is to slowly increase the amount of time your dog has to pinpoint, his nose in the hole, from one to five seconds or even more before you throw the ball.

If your dog understands what he has to do with the scent-laden box, bring another, identical box to the training place and put the boxes in a line-up. One has the scent and the other doesn't. Always use the same box for the odor substances, otherwise you run the risk of all your boxes acquiring the scent, and your dog will end up pinpointing every box.

Bring your dog over to the line-up in such a way that he first meets the box without any scent and then the one with the scent. Now you will see if the training has been correct. If your dog sits at the first box and brings his nose to the hole, you have to go back to the initial training, because he didn't understand that he is not supposed to sit and bring his nose down at any box, but only at boxes where he smells the odor.

If your dog worked out the mini-line-up well—so, he sniffed the first box and moved on to the second, where he sniffed, sat, and put his nose to the hole—throw the ball and reward him. After a while, you can start using three or four boxes, or even more. Be sure to regularly change the position of the scented box in the line-up.

If everything goes well, you can progress to putting the boxes in corners of the room and asking your dog to search for the correct box, sit, and pinpoint. If he does this correctly, take out the container or wrapping that encloses the scent in the box and hide that at the same spot it was the last time you practiced. Your dog should approach the place where he can smell the hidden scent container/wrappings, and he should sniff, sit, and pinpoint.

Finally, you can practice this exercise in different rooms, using different hiding places—in other houses, cars, outbuildings, and places where your dog will have to work in his career as a detector dog. Always slowly build up the training until your dog can find the substances anywhere and give a correct passive response.

Responses

Following are the specific responses suitable for certain jobs.

1. *Arson-Detector Dogs* Active (scratching, barking) or passive alert (with pinpointing).
2. *Cadaver-Detector Dogs* Active alert (scratching and barking).
3. *Disease- (Skin Cancer, and so on) Detector Dogs* Active alert (sniffing, wagging, barking).
4. *Drug-Detector Dogs* Active alert for dogs searching in ships or containers; active (barking) or passive (with pinpointing) for dogs searching in and around vehicles, homes, parcels, and luggage; passive (without pinpointing) for control of people (passengers and staff).
5. *Epilepsy-Detector Dogs* Active alert (a special bark).
6. *Explosives-Detector Dogs* Passive alert (without pinpointing) for explosives and bombs; passive or active (barking) for arms and ammunition; active (bringsel) for explosives and arms.
7. *Gas-Detector Dogs* Active alert (scratching, biting, barking).
8. *Mold-Detector Dogs ("Rothounds")* Active alert.
9. *Ore-Deposit-Search Dogs* Active alert (barking, scratching).

10. *Search-and-Rescue Dogs* Active alert (barking, scratching, bringsel) for finding people alive; passive (with pinpointing) for finding dead bodies.
11. *Tobacco-Detector Dogs* Active alert for searching in ships, containers, vehicles, and buildings.
12. *Truffle-Search Dogs* Active alert (scratching).

Searching Homes and Buildings

Searching a house, office, or warehouse is often difficult for detector dogs and their handlers. Generally, the area to be covered is extensive and distracting influences are numerous. Detailed preparation and systematic execution of proven search techniques are required if the team is to achieve success. During these searches, your control of your dog is very important. You must curb your dog's natural tendency to explore and probe at random, and your dog must not be allowed to roam freely.

Wind conditions are extremely difficult to assess when working indoors. Drafts, cross-ventilation, and heating and air-conditioning units all affect existing scent patterns. You must control these conditions as much as possible by switching off air conditioners and heaters. Despite all efforts to control the working environment, however, wind and internal drafts will continue to affect your dog's keen sense of smell. These conditions may result in seemingly false alerts, positive alerts accompanied by an inability to pinpoint the source, and general alerts on airborne scent throughout the building.

If your dog indicates a general alert throughout a building—barking at several places in the room, or against walls, sometimes with his nose held high in the air—two things could be happening. Either the substance is hidden in the air-conditioning or heating system, or there is so much odor in the building that your dog cannot make a detailed search for it. If the latter is the case, open the doors and windows and allow your dog to go outside (even outside the building) to get a breath of fresh air. After that, and

If we could only know what our dogs know, we could enormously increase our potential for scent detection.

perhaps after taking even more breaks outside, he should be able to pinpoint the odor source.

A more difficult situation comes up if your dog alerts downwind from the hiding place. In this case, you must be extremely careful in administering correction or praise. Where a draft is obviously present, encourage your dog to work back upwind in an attempt to pinpoint the source. This requires you to search all areas as you and your dog move back upwind. If you direct adequate verbal encouragement at your dog, this technique should be successful.

As you guide your dog through the search area, use initiative, never overlook the obvious, and show your dog each area to be checked.

Observe your dog carefully for evidence of an alert. If a situation appears doubtful, follow your dog's instincts rather than attempt to rationalize it from a human point of view.

If there is doubt, respect your dog's instincts.

The following guidance is applicable when searching any room, regardless of size, function, or configuration.

SEARCHING A ROOM

1. Prior to commencing search operations, your dog should be allowed to become familiar with his surroundings, such as slippery floors. If possible, the area should be cleared of personnel and pets and other distracting influences minimized. Be on the alert for dangerous materials such as syringes, chemicals, food, and so on.

2. You, the handler, should mentally divide each room into equal quarters with a view to searching each quarter in an orderly fashion. Then your dog has to start a systematic screening of the area.

3. If noticeable wind currents or internal drafts are present, move your dog downwind and let him search for airborne scent.

4. In training, you taught your dog to search "Low" and "High." Use these commands and help him by touching or pointing at the items you want your dog to search. When searching areas that are higher up (shelves, for example), you can use a table to boost your dog.

5. Baseboards, ventilation ducts, sockets, bookcases, and other furniture or equipment along the walls and ceiling should be checked first. Once these items have been cleared, your team can move systematically to other items contained in that particular quadrant and conduct a detailed screening of them.

6. If your dog gives a false alert, make certain he wasn't responding to a residual scent. It's possible, after all, that the substance you are looking for may have been hidden in that location recently. You can check on this with a tissue and special sprays (for instance, for drugs).
7. When the alert is valid, always consider the possibility that there are more hiding places in the same quarter (near or behind each other).
8. After you and your dog have carefully searched each quarter of the room, announce that the area is clear. Then, proceed to the next room and continue searching until the search is complete.

Searching Animal Barns

Searches in barns or kennels are not the simplest ones, either, but they can be done. In spite of the strong scents of fertilizer and animal manure, your dog should have no problem finding what he needs to find in barns or kennels, or on farm grounds in general. Depending on your dog's reaction to them, cattle can stay in the barn. It is very interesting to watch a well-trained dog searching among cattle.

Searching Open Terrain

Detector dogs can also search for buried containers and dig them up, when they are trained to do so. You cannot know how deeply your dog can smell into the ground for a given substance until you give it a try. Weather and the soil conditions are very important here and can affect the search in a positive or negative way, as does the strength of the odor, the packing material around the substance, and any other masking agents.

Searching Populated Areas

People, traffic, foreign odors, other animals, loud noises, and strange objects tend to divert detector dogs' attention from their primary task. In some cases you, the handler, may also be tempted to relax your vigilance in the face of many distractions. However, your team's ability to function effectively under such circumstances is of paramount importance. Employ basic obedience, scent discrimination, and systematic techniques to reduce the impact of distracting influences. When searching populated areas, follow the guidelines listed below whenever possible.

1. Have faith in yourself and your dog.
2. Analyze the search area before you commit your dog to the search.
3. Allow your dog to familiarize himself with the area before searching.
4. Identify potential trouble spots at the outset and report them immediately.
5. If possible, eliminate or minimize distracting influences.
6. When distractions cannot be reduced significantly, work slowly, exercise firm control over your dog, and encourage him to perform the task required.
7. Adhere to established search techniques and require your dog to do so, too.
8. Don't rationalize the legitimacy of a particular situation. Everyone and everything is suspect. If there is doubt, your dog's instinct, not yours, should be respected.
9. Logic, common sense, and sound dog-handling practices are required at all times to successfully accomplish the search mission. If you employ these skills properly, working in populated areas will present no major problems for you and your dog.

Searching Vehicles

For this type of search, you must exercise firm control on your dog at all times. Also, be careful not to read a false alert, as vehicles have much extraneous scent in and around them. Human- and animal-associated odors may confuse your dog and distract him from the search. Vehicle searches should be conducted in exactly the same manner each time. This is not always possible with other types of searches. If you employ the following techniques, you should not encounter any significant problems when searching vehicles.

1. Close all vehicle doors and open the hood and trunk.
2. First, quarter your dog downwind of the vehicle. If no alert occurs, proceed directly to the front of the vehicle and commence searching in a clockwise direction. Make sure fenders, wheels, hubcaps, bumpers, quarter panels, and the undercarriage receive careful screening.
3. Search the trunk and engine compartment next. If the engine is still warm, put a piece of carpet over it. Besides protecting your dog from a potential burn, the carpet gives him a comfortable place to stand.
4. Terminate the search with a careful examination of the vehicle interior. This includes seats, floorboards, dashboard, ashtrays, armrests, headrests, seat belts, and accessories. For this type of search, smaller detector dogs (such as spaniels) are very suitable.
5. Luggage may be removed from the trunk or interior of the vehicle and searched separately.

Vehicle searches are particularly difficult for some dogs because they must negotiate certain obstacles to accomplish the mission. Encourage your dog to jump into the trunk, crawl under the vehicle, and search high into the engine compartment.

Searching Ships

Searching ships is definitely not easy. In the first place, there are a lot of hiding places, rooms, cabins, and passages, and it's difficult to stay oriented and remember where your dog has already searched. Passing through all of a ship's spaces is often hard going and requires some adjustment and special efforts on the part of you and your dog. Having to crawl under and over pipes, walk on open stairs, and negotiate insecure footing and cramped working conditions may create problems for your dog. Detector dogs also have to deal with the fact that the ship doesn't stay still; however, they will get used to that after a while. Such conditions can be overcome only by concentration, patience, repetition, and your encouragement.

Training Problems

Following are the problems in training that we see over and over again and that can affect your dog's success as a detector dog.

1. Moving forward too quickly while training beginners.
2. Not working out the different steps in an exercise thoroughly or enough times.
3. Too many distractions in the initial training.
4. Too little enthusiasm on the part of the handler.
5. The handler keeps the ball (or another reward) in his hand—in clear view of the dog—while the dog searches, thus distracting him.
6. The handler always uses the same hiding and training places.
7. The handler uses contaminated odor substances and other bad training materials.

General Problems

Following are the main problems we have seen handlers and their dogs encounter in practice.

1. The handler gives the dog too little time to work out the scent clue.
2. The search area is poorly or non-ventilated.
3. There is too much noise in the vicinity of the searching dog.
4. Too many people are milling around in the search area.
5. People are smoking in the rooms to be searched.
6. The handler has not removed dangers for the dog (syringes, broken glass).

7. The handler shows too little or no interest in the matter.
8. The handler is nervous or impatient.
9. The dog is tired from searching for too long a period.
10. The dog is under too much pressure to perform—too much is expected from him.

The Biggest Problem

In implementing our training method for detector dogs (with both active and passive alerts), we see that after some training and explanation, handlers look at their dogs in a different way and also handle their dogs differently. They no longer see their dogs as objects to train but instead have learned that their dogs are full partners in the task at hand.

The biggest problem with the training of all kinds of search dogs is always the handler, who, shaped by his or her environment, first has to understand the difference between commanded, mechanical dog training, and the intricate work involved with training search dogs. Once the handler has grasped that difference, he or she can switch to a new way of thinking about dogs. When the handler has overcome this hurdle, handler and dog can be a good team: two colleagues, each with a particular specialty.

Two colleagues, each with his own specialty.

Notes

Introduction

1. See N. Nicolaides and J.M.B. Apon, "The Saturated Methyl Branched Fatty Acids of Adult Human Skin Surface Lipid," *Biomedical Mass Spectrometry* 5, no.6 (1977): 337–47. See also B.A. Sommerville, M.A. Green, and D.J. Gee, "Using Chromatography and a Dog to Identify Some of the Compounds in Human Sweat which Are Under Genetic Influence," in *Chemical Signals in Vertebrates*, 5th ed., ed. D.W. Macdonald et al. (Oxford: Oxford University Press, 1990), 634–39. And see U.R. Bernier, D.L. Kline, D.R. Barnard, C.E. Schreck, and R.A. Yost, "Analysis of Human Skin Emanations by Gas Chromatography/Mass Spectrometry," *Analytical Chemistry* 72, no. 4 (February 15, 2000): 747–56.

Living in Different Worlds

1. Our translation of J. Von Uexküll and G. Kriszat, *Streifzüge durch die Umwelten von Tieren und Menschen* (Berlin: Verständliche Wissenschaft, XXI, 1934), 5–7.
2. Our translation of F.J.J. Buytendijk, *De Psychologie van den Hond* (Amsterdam: Uitgeverij Kosmos, 1932), 64–67.
3. D.J. Stierman, "Animals 'Hear' Quakes," *The San Bernardino County Sun*, June 8, 1979, 28.
4. A.C. Lawson, *The Californian Earthquake of April 18, 1906* (American Commission of Investigation, 1906), 382.
5. P. Vroon, *Zonder Geur Geen Emoties* (Amsterdam: De Volkskrant, 1989), 23.
6. Oliver Sacks, *The Man Who Mistook His Wife for a Hat and Other Clinical Tales* (New York: Touchstone Books, 1985).
7. R. Menzel and R. Menzel, *Pariahunde* (Wittenberg Lutherstadt: A. Ziemsen Verlag, 1960).
8. H. Stephan, "Die Anwendung der Schnell'schen Formel h=ks.p auf Hirn-Körpergewichtsbeziehungen bei verschiedene Hunderassen," *Zoologischer Anzeiger* 153 (1954): 15–27.

9 J. Bodingbauer, *Das Wunder der Hundenase* (Vienna: Unsere Hunde, 1977).
10 B. Schaal, P. Orgeur, and C. Arnould, "Olfactory Preferences in Newborn Lambs: Possible Influence of Prenatal Experience," *Behaviour* 132, nos. 5–6 (1995): 351–65. See also, B. Schaal, L. Marlier, and R. Soussignan, "Responsiveness to the Odour of Amniotic Fluid in the Human Neonate," *Biology of the Neonate* 67, no. 6 (1995): 397–406.
11 E. Semke, H. Distel, and R. Hudson, "Specific Enhancement of Olfactory Receptor Sensitivity Associated with Foetal Learning of Food Odors in the Rabbit," *Naturwissenschaften* 82 (1995): 148–49.
12 P.G. Hepper, "Long-Term Retention of Kinship Recognition Established During Infancy in the Domestic Dog," *Behavioural Processes* 33 (1994): 14.
13 R.E. Lubow, M. Kahn, and R. Frommer, "Information Processing of Olfactory Stimuli by the Dog: I. The Acquisition and Retention of Four Odor-Pair Discriminations," *Bulletin of the Psychonomic Society* 1, no. 2 (1973): 143–45.

Human Odor on Objects

1 J. Bodingbauer, *Das Wunder der Hundenase* (Vienna: Unsere Hunde, 1977).
2 D.G. Moulton, "Minimum Odorant Concentrations Detectable by the Dog and Their Implications for Olfactory Receptor Sensitivity," in *Chemical Signals in Vertebrates*, eds. D. Müller-Schwarz and M.M. Mozell (New York, London: Plenum, 1977), 455–64.
3 G.E. Schwartz, I.R. Bell, Z.V. Dikman, M. Fernandez, J.P. Kline, and J.M. Peterson, "EEG Responses to Low-Level Chemicals in Normals and Cacosmics," *Toxicology and Industrial Health* 10, nos. 4–5 (1995): 633–43.
4 D.M. Stoddart, *The Scented Ape: The Biology and Culture of Human Odour* (Cambridge: Cambridge University Press, 1990), 102–115.
5 A.I. Spielman, X.N. Zeng, J.J. Leden, and G. Preti, "Proteinaceous Precursors of Human Axillary Odor: Isolation of Two Novel Odor-binding Proteins," *Experientia* 51, no. 1 (January 15, 1995): 40–47.
6 E.A. Eady, M.R. Farmery, J.I. Ross, J.H. Cove, and W.J. Cunliffe, "Effects of Benzoyl Peroxide and Erythromycin Alone and in Combination against Antibiotic-Sensitive and -Resistant Skin Bacteria from Acne Patients," *British Journal of Dermatology* 131, no. 3 (September 1994): 331–36. See also M.E. Stewart and D.T. Downing, "Chemistry and Function of Mammalian Sebaceous Lipids," *Advances in Lipid Research* 24 (1991): 263–301.
7 H.C. Korting, A. Lukacs, and O. Braun-Falco, "Microbial Flora and Odor of the Healthy Human Skin," *Hautarzt* 39, no. 9 (September 1988): 564–68.
8 C is a prefix in the metric system denoting a factor of one hundredth (10^{-2}).
9 R.S. Ramotowski, "Composition of Latent Fingerprint Residue," in *Advances in Fingerprint Technology*, ed. H.C. Lee and R.E. Gaensslen (Boca Raton, FL: CRC Press, 2001).
10 L. Bonifort, S. Passi, F. Caprilli, and M. Nazarro-Porro, "Skin Surface Lipids: Identification and Determination by Thin-layer Chromatography and Gas-liquid Chromatography," *Clinica Chemica Acta* 47, no. 2 (August 30, 1973): 223–31.
11 S.C. Green, M.E. Stewart, and D.T. Downing, "Variation in Sebum Fatty Acid Composition among Adult Humans," *Journal of Investigative Dermatology* 83 (1984): 114–17.

12 Ibid.
13 M.E. Stewart, M.W. McDonnell, and D.T. Downing, "Possible Genetic Control of the Proportions of Branched-Chain Fatty Acids in Human Sebaceous Wax Esters," *Journal of Investigative Dermatology* 86 (1986): 706–708.
14 Z.T. Halpin, "Individual Odors among Mammals: Origins and Functions," *Advances in the Study of Behavior* 16 (1986): 39–70.
15 E.A. Boyse, "HLA and the Chemical Senses," *Human Immunology*, 15, no. 4 (1986): 391–95.
16 L. Löhner, "Über menschliche Individual- und Regionalgerüche," *European Journal of Physiology* 202 (1924).
17 Stoddart, *The Scented Ape*, 135.
18 C. Wedekind and S. Furi, "Body Odour Preferences in Men and Women: Do They Aim for Specific MHC Combinations or Simply Heterozygosity?" *Proceedings of the Royal Society B: Biological Sciences* (1997).
19 Ramotowski, "Composition," 63–104.
20 A. Schoon, "The Performance of Dogs in Identifying Humans by Scent" (PhD diss. Leiden, 1997).
21 R.M. Wilcox and R.E. Johnston, "Scent Counter-Marks: Specialised Mechanisms of Perception and Response to Individual Odors in Golden Hamsters (*Mesocricetus auratus*)," *Journal of Comparative Psychology* 109, no. 4 (1995): 349–56. See also R.E. Johnston, E.S. Soroking, and M.H. Ferkin, "Scent Counter-Marking in Meadow Voles: Females Prefer the Top-Scent Male," *Ethology* 103, no. 6 (1997): 443–53.
22 H. Kalmus, "The Discrimination by the Nose of the Dog of Individual Human Odours and in Particular of the Odours of Twins," *British Journal of Animal Behaviour* 5 (January 1955).
23 L. Löhner, "Über menschliche Individual- und Regionalgerüche," *European Journal of Physiology* 202 (1924).
24 M. Rogowski, "Possibility of Removing the Individual Scent with the Aid of Clothes" (paper presented at the conference Osmology: Overestimated or Neglected Area of Forensic Science? *Problemy Kryminalistyki* 230 [2000]: 56–58).

Human Odor on a Track

1 W. Neuhaus, "Über die Riechschärfe des Hundes für Fettsäuren," *Zeitschrift für vergleichende Physiologie* 35 (1953): 527–52.
2 W. Neuhaus, "Die Unterscheidungsfähigkeit des Hundes für Duftgemische," *Zeitschrift für vergleichende Physiologie* 39(1956): 25–43.
3 W.G. Syrotuck, *Scent and the Scenting Dog* (Westmoreland: Arner Publications, 1972), 30.
4 F. Kanda, E. Yagi, M. Fukuda, K. Nakajima, T. Ohta, and O. Nakato, "Elucidation of Chemical Compounds Responsible for Foot Malodour," *British Journal of Dermatology* 122, no. 6 (1990): 771–76.

The Dog's Nose

1 J. Bodingbauer, *Das Wunder der Hundenase* (Vienna: Unsere Hunde, 1977).
2 K.A. Wagner, *Rezente Hunderassen: Eine osteologische Untersuchung* (Oslo: J. Dybwad Publisher, 1930).

3 W. Neuhaus, "Die Bedeutung des Schnüffelns für das Riechen des Hundes," *Zeitung für Säugetierkunde* 46, no. 5 (1981): 301–10.
4 D. Lancet, "Vertebrate Olfactory Reception," *Annual Review of Neuroscience* 9 (1986): 329–55.
5 S.H. Snyder, P.B. Sklar, and J. Pevsner, "Molecular Mechanisms of Olfaction," *The Journal of Biological Chemistry* 263, no. 28 (1988): 13971–74. See also K. Mori, and Y. Yoshihara, "Molecular Recognition and Olfactory Processing in the Mammalian Olfactory System," *Progress in Neurobiology* 45 (1995): 585–619.
6 D. Lancet, "Exclusive Receptors," *Nature* 372 (1994): 321–22.
7 J. Boeckh, "Die chemischen Sinne, Geruch und Geschmack," in *Physiologie des Menschen (Sinnesphysiologie I), Somatische Sensibilität und chemische Sinne*, eds. Kramer, Gauer, Jung (München-Berlin-Wien: Schwarzenberg, 1970), 169–231.
8 M.D. Pearsall, and H. Verbruggen, *Scent: Training to Track, Search and Rescue* (Loveland: Alpine Publications, 1982).
9 P. Pelosi, "Odorant-Binding Proteins," *Critical Reviews in Biochemistry and Molecular Biology* 29, no. 3 (1994): 199–228.
10 D.G. Moulton, "Minimum Odorant Concentrations Detectable by the Dog and Their Implications for Olfactory Receptor Sensitivity," in *Chemical Signals in Vertebrates*, eds. D. Müller-Schwarz and M.M. Mozell (New York, London: Plenum, 1977), 455–64.
11 V.B. Droscher, *The Magic of the Senses* (London: W. H. Allen; New York: Dutton, 1967).
12 B.M. Kavoi and H. Jameela, "Comparative Morphometry of the Olfactory Bulb, Tract and Stria in the Human, Dog and Goat," *International Journal of Morphology* 29, no. 3 (2011): 939–46.
13 R.W. Moncrieff, *The Chemical Senses* (London: Leonard Hill, 1951).
14 W. Neuhaus, "Die Unterscheidung von Duftquantitäten bei Mensch und Hund nach Versuchen mit Buttersäure," *Zeitschrift für vergleichende Physiologie* 37 (1955): 234–52.
15 Y. Yeshurun and N. Sobel, "An Odor Is Not Worth a Thousand Words: From Multidimensional Odors to Unidimensional Odor Objects," *Annual Review of Psychology* 61 (2010): 219–41.
16 T. Lord and M. Kasprzak, "Identification of Self through Olfaction," *Perceptual Motor Skills* 69 (1989): 219–24.
17 R.H. Porter, J.M. Cernoch, and F.J. McLaughlin, "Maternal Recognition of Neonates through Olfactory Cues," *Physiology and Behavior* 30 (1983): 151–54.
18 B. Schaal, H. Montagner, E. Hertling, D. Bolzoni, A. Moyse, and R. Quichon, "Olfactory Stimulations in Mother–Child Relations," *Reproduction Nutrition Development* 20 (1980): 843–58.
19 K.R. Hovis, R. Ramnath, J.E. Dahlen, A.L. Romanova, G. LaRocca, M.E. Bier, and N.N. Urban, "Activity Regulates Functional Connectivity from the Vomeronasal Organ to the Accessory Olfactory Bulb," *Journal of Neuroscience* 32, no. 23 (June 2012): 7907–16.
20 J. Porter, B. Craven, R.M. Khan, S.J. Chang, I. Kang, B. Judkewitz, J. Volpe, G. Settles, and N. Sobel, "Mechanisms of Scent-tracking in Humans," *Natural Neuroscience* 10, no. 1 (January 2007): 27–29.
21 L. Lee Sela, and N. Sobel, "Human Olfaction: A Constant State of Change-Blindness," *Experimental Brain Research* 205, no. 1 (August 2010): 13–29.

Odors and Perception

1. K. Zuschneid, "Die Riechleistung des Hundes" (PhD diss. Berlin, 1973).
2. S. Silbernagl and A. Despopoulos, *Color Atlas of Physiology*, 6th Edition (New York: Thieme Medical Publications, 2008), 344–61.
3. D. Lancet, "Exclusive Receptors," *Nature* 372 (1994): 321–22.
4. H.W. Wang, C.J. Wysocki, and G.H. Gold, "Induction of Olfactory Receptor Sensitivity in Mice," *Science* 260, no. 5110 (May 14, 1993): 998–1000. And S.L. Youngentob and P.F. Kent, "Enhancement of Odorant-Induced Mucosal Activity Patterns in Rats Trained on an Odorant Identification Task," *Brain Research* 670, no. 1 (1995): 82–88.
5. R. Gross-Isseroff and D. Lancet, "Concentration Dependent Changes of Perceived Odor Quality," *Chemical Senses* 13, no. 2 (1988): 191–204.
6. K. Mori and Y. Yoshihara, "Molecular Recognition and Olfactory Processing in the Mammalian Olfactory System," *Progress in Neurobiology* 45 (1995): 585–619.
7. M. Laska and R. Hudson, "Discriminating Parts from a Whole: Determinants of Odor Mixture Perception in Squirrel Monkeys, *Saimiri Sciureus*," *Journal of Comparative Physiology* 173, no. 2 (1993): 249–56.
8. D.G. Laing, H. Panhuber, and B.M. Slotnick, "Odor Masking in the Rat," *Physiology & Behavior* 45 (1989): 689–94. See also D.G. Laing, A. Eddy, and D.J. Best, "Perceptual Characteristics of Binary, Trinary, and Quaternary Odor Mixtures," *Physiology & Behavior* 56, no. 1 (1994): 81–93.
9. J.D. Pierce, X.N. Zeng, E.V. Aronov, G. Preti, and C.J. Wysocki, "Cross-Adaptation of Sweaty-Smelling 3-Methyl-2-Hexonoic Acid by a Structurally Similar, Pleasant Smelling Odorant," *Chemical Senses* 20, no. 4 (1995): 401–11.
10. P. Vroon, *Zonder Geur Geen Emoties* (Amsterdam: De Volkskrant, 1989), 23.

Bibliography

Bodingbauer, J. 1977. *Das Wunder der Hundenase*. Vienna: Unsere Hunde.

Boeckh, J. "Die Chemischen Sinne, Geruch und Geschmack." In *Physiologie des Menschen (Sinnesphysiologie I), Somatische Sensibilität und Chemische Sinne,* edited by Kramer, Gauer, Jung, 169–231. München-Berlin-Wien: Schwarzenberg, 1970.

Bonifort, L., S. Passi, F. Caprilli, and M. Nazarro-Porro. 30 August 1973. "Skin Surface Lipids: Identification and Determination by Thin-layer Chromatography and Gas-liquid Chromatography." *Clinica Chimica Acta* 47 (2): 223–231. http://dx.doi.org/10.1016/0009-8981(73)90319-7.

Boyse, E.A. 1986. "HLA and the Chemical Senses." *Human Immunology* 15 (4): 391–395. http://dx.doi.org/10.1016/0198-8859(86)90016-9.

Droscher, V.B. 1967. *The Magic of the Senses*. London: W. H. Allen. New York: Dutton.

Eady, E.A., M.R. Farmery, J.I. Ross, J.H. Cove, and W.J. Cunliffe. September 1994. "Effects of Benzoyl Peroxide and Erythromycin Alone and in Combination against Antibiotic-Sensitive and -Resistant Skin Bacteria from Acne Patients." *British Journal of Dermatology* 131 (3): 331–336. http://dx.doi.org/10.1111/j.1365-2133.1994.tb08519.x.

Green, S.C., M.E. Stewart, and D.T. Downing. 1984. "Variation in Sebum Fatty Acid Composition among Adult Humans." *Journal of Investigative Dermatology* 83 (2): 114–117. http://dx.doi.org/10.1111/1523-1747.ep12263287.

Gross-Isseroff, R., and D. Lancet. 1988. "Concentration Dependent Changes of Perceived Odor Quality." *Chemical Senses* 13 (2): 191–204. http://dx.doi.org/10.1093/chemse/13.2.191.

Halpin, Z.T. 1986. "Individual Odors among Mammals: Origins and Functions." *Advances in the Study of Behavior* 16:39–70. http://dx.doi.org/10.1016/S0065-3454(08)60187-4.

Hepper, P.G. 1994. "Long-Term Retention of Kinship Recognition Established During Infancy in the Domestic Dog." *Behavioural Processes* 33 (1-2): 3–14. http://dx.doi.org/10.1016/0376-6357(94)90056-6.

Hovis, K.R., R. Ramnath, J.E. Dahlen, et al. June 2012. "Activity Regulates Functional Connectivity from the Vomeronasal Organ to the Accessory Olfactory Bulb." *Journal of Neuroscience* 32 (23): 7907–7916. http://dx.doi.org/10.1523/JNEUROSCI.2399-11.2012.

Johnston, R.E., E.S. Soroking, and M.H. Ferkin. 1997. "Scent Counter-Marking in Meadow Voles: Females Prefer the Top-Scent Male." *Ethology* 103 (6): 443–453. http://dx.doi.org/10.1111/j.1439-0310.1997.tb00159.x.

Kalmus, H. January 1955. "The Discrimination by the Nose of the Dog of Individual Human Odours and in Particular of the Odours of Twins." *British Journal of Animal Behaviour* 5.

Kanda, F., E. Yagi, M. Fukuda, K. Nakajima, T. Ohta, and O. Nakato. 1990. "Elucidation of Chemical Compounds Responsible for Foot Malodour." *British Journal of Dermatology* 122 (6): 771–776. http://dx.doi.org/10.1111/j.1365-2133.1990.tb06265.x.

Kavoi, B.M., and H. Jameela. 2011. "Comparative Morphometry of the Olfactory Bulb, Tract and Stria in the Human, Dog and Goat." *International Journal of Morphology* 29 (3): 939–946. http://dx.doi.org/10.4067/S0717-95022011000300047.

Korting, H.C., A. Lukacs, and O. Braun-Falco. September 1988. "Microbial Flora and Odor of the Healthy Human Skin." *Der Hautarzt* 39 (9): 564–568.

Laing, D.G., A. Eddy, and D.J. Best. 1994. "Perceptual Characteristics of Binary, Trinary, and Quaternary Odor Mixtures." *Physiology & Behavior* 56 (1): 81–93. http://dx.doi.org/10.1016/0031-9384(94)90264-X.

Laing, D.G., H. Panhuber, and B.M. Slotnick. 1989. "Odor Masking in the Rat." *Physiology & Behavior* 45 (4): 689–694. http://dx.doi.org/10.1016/0031-9384(89)90280-1.

Lancet, D. 1994. "Olfaction. Exclusive Receptors." *Nature* 372 (6504): 321–322. http://dx.doi.org/10.1038/372321a0.

Lancet, D. 1986. "Vertebrate Olfactory Reception." *Annual Review of Neuroscience* 9 (1): 329–355. http://dx.doi.org/10.1146/annurev.ne.09.030186.001553.

Laska, M., and R. Hudson. 1993. "Discriminating Parts from a Whole: Determinants of Odor Mixture Perception in Squirrel Monkeys, *Saimiri Sciureus*." *Journal of Comparative Physiology* 173 (2): 249–256.

Lawson, A.C. 1906. *The Californian Earthquake of April 18, 1906*. American Commission of Investigation.

Löhner, L. 1924. "Über menschliche Individual- und Regionalgerüche." *European Journal of Physiology* 202 (1): 25–45. http://dx.doi.org/10.1007/BF01723477.

Lord, T., and M. Kasprzak. 1989. "Identification of Self through Olfaction." *Perceptual and Motor Skills* 69 (1): 219–224. http://dx.doi.org/10.2466/pms.1989.69.1.219.

Lubow, R.E., M. Kahn, and R. Frommer. 1973. "Information Processing of Olfactory Stimuli by the Dog: I. The Acquisition and Retention of Four

Odor-Pair Discriminations." *Bulletin of the Psychonomic Society* 1 (2): 143–145. http://dx.doi.org/10.3758/BF03334324.

Menzel, R. and R. Menzel. 1960. *Pariahunde*. Wittenberg Lutherstadt: A. Ziemsen Verlag.

Moncrieff, R.W. 1951. *The Chemical Senses*. London: Leonard Hill.

Mori, K., and Y. Yoshihara. 1995. "Molecular Recognition and Olfactory Processing in the Mammalian Olfactory System." *Progress in Neurobiology* 45 (6): 585–619. http://dx.doi.org/10.1016/0301-0082(94)00058-P.

Moulton, D.G. 1977. "Minimum Odorant Concentrations Detectable by the Dog and Their Implications for Olfactory Receptor Sensitivity." In *Chemical Signals in Vertebrates*, ed. D. Müller-Schwarz and M.M. Mozell, 455–464. New York, London: Plenum. http://dx.doi.org/10.1007/978-1-4684-2364-8_25.

Neuhaus, W. 1981. "Die Bedeutung des Schnüffelns für das Riechen des Hundes." *Zeitung für Säugetierkunde* 46 (5): 301–310.

———. 1953. "Über die Riechschärfe des Hundes für Fettsäuren." *Zeitschrift für Vergleichende Physiologie* 35:527–552.

———. 1955. "Die Unterscheidung von Duftquantitäten bei Mensch und Hund nach Versuchen mit Buttersäure." *Zeitschrift für Vergleichende Physiologie* 37 (3): 234–252. http://dx.doi.org/10.1007/BF00298313.

Nicolaides, N., and J.M.B. Apon. 1977. "The Saturated Methyl Branched Fatty Acids of Adult Human Skin Surface Lipid." *Biomedical Mass Spectrometry* 4 (6): 337–347. http://dx.doi.org/10.1002/bms.1200040604.

Pearsall, M.D., and H. Verbruggen. 1982. *Scent: Training to Track, Search, and Rescue*. Loveland, CO: Alpine Publications.

Pelosi, P. 1994. "Odorant-Binding Proteins." *Critical Reviews in Biochemistry and Molecular Biology* 29 (3): 199–228. http://dx.doi.org/10.3109/10409239409086801.

Pierce, J.D., Jr., X.N. Zeng, E.V. Aronov, G. Preti, and C.J. Wysocki. 1995. "Cross-Adaptation of Sweaty-Smelling 3-Methyl-2-Hexonoic Acid by a Structurally Similar, Pleasant Smelling Odorant." *Chemical Senses* 20 (4): 401–411. http://dx.doi.org/10.1093/chemse/20.4.401.

Porter, J., B. Craven, R.M. Khan, et al. January 2007. "Mechanisms of Scent-tracking in Humans." *Nature Neuroscience* 10 (1): 27–29. http://dx.doi.org/10.1038/nn1819.

Porter, R.H., J.M. Cernoch, and F.J. McLaughlin. 1983. "Maternal Recognition of Neonates through Olfactory Cues." *Physiology & Behavior* 30 (1): 151–154. http://dx.doi.org/10.1016/0031-9384(83)90051-3.

Ramotowski, R.S. 2001. "Composition of Latent Fingerprint Residue." In *Advances in Fingerprint Technology*, ed. H.C. Lee and R.E. Gaensslen. Boca Raton, FL: CRC Press. http://dx.doi.org/10.1201/9781420041347.ch3.

Rogowski, M. 2000. "Possibility of Removing the Individual Scent with the Aid of Clothes." Paper presented at the conference Osmology: Overestimated or Neglected Area of Forensic Science? *Problemy Kryminalistyki* 230: 56–58.

Sacks, Oliver. 1998. *The Man Who Mistook His Wife for a Hat and Other Clinical Tales*. New York: Touchstone Books.

Schaal, B., L. Marlier, and R. Soussignan. 1995. "Responsiveness to the Odour of Amniotic Fluid in the Human Neonate." *Biology of the Neonate* 67 (6): 397–406. http://dx.doi.org/10.1159/000244192.

Schaal, B., H. Montagner, E. Hertling, D. Bolzoni, A. Moyse, and R. Quichon. 1980. "Olfactory Stimulations in Mother–Child Relations." *Reproduction, Nutrition, Development* 20:843–858. http://dx.doi.org/10.1051/rnd:19800510.

Schaal, B., P. Orgeur, and C. Arnould. 1995. "Olfactory Preferences in Newborn Lambs: Possible Influence of Prenatal Experience." *Behaviour* 132 (5–6): 351–365. http://dx.doi.org/10.1163/156853995X00603.

Schoon, A. "The Performance of Dogs in Identifying Humans by Scent." PhD diss., Leiden, 1997.

Schwartz, G.E., I.R. Bell, Z.V. Dikman, M. Fernandez, J.P. Kline, and J.M. Peterson. 1995. "EEG Responses to Low-Level Chemicals in Normals and Cacosmics." *Toxicology and Industrial Health* 10 (4–5): 633–643.

Sela, L., and N. Sobel. August 2010. "Human Olfaction: A Constant State of Change-Blindness." *Experimental Brain Research* 205 (1): 13–29. http://dx.doi.org/10.1007/s00221-010-2348-6.

Semke, E., H. Distel, and R. Hudson. 1995. "Specific Enhancement of Olfactory Receptor Sensitivity Associated with Foetal Learning of Food Odors in the Rabbit." *Naturwissenschaften* 82 (3): 148–149. http://dx.doi.org/10.1007/BF01177279.

Silbernagl, S., and A. Despopoulos. 2008. *Color Atlas of Physiology*. 6th ed. New York: Thieme Medical Publications.

Snyder, S.H., P.B. Sklar, and J. Pevsner. 1988. "Molecular Mechanisms of Olfaction." *Journal of Biological Chemistry* 263 (28): 13971–13974.

Spielman, A.I., X.N. Zeng, J.J. Leden, and G. Preti. 15 January 1995. "Proteinaceous Precursors of Human Axillary Odor: Isolation of Two Novel Odorbinding Proteins." *Experientia* 51 (1): 40–47.

Stephan, H. 1954. "Die Anwendung der Schnell'schen Formel h=ks.p auf Hirn-Körpergewichtsbeziehungen bei verschiedene Hunderassen." *Zoologischer Anzeiger* 153:15–27.

Stewart, M.E., and D.T. Downing. 1991. "Chemistry and Function of Mammalian Sebaceous Lipids." *Advances in Lipid Research* 24:263–301. http://dx.doi.org/10.1016/B978-0-12-024924-4.50013-4.

Stewart, M.E., M.W. McDonnell, and D.T. Downing. 1986. "Possible Genetic Control of the Proportions of Branched-Chain Fatty Acids in Human Sebaceous Wax Esters." *Journal of Investigative Dermatology* 86 (6): 706–708. http://dx.doi.org/10.1111/1523-1747.ep12276326.

Stoddary, D.M. 1990. *The Scented Ape: The Biology and Culture of Human Odour*. Cambridge: Cambridge University Press.

Sommerville, B.A., M.A. Green, and D.J. Gee. 1990. "Using Chromatography and a Dog to Identify Some of the Compounds in Human Sweat which Are Under Genetic Influence." In *Chemical Signals in Vertebrates*, 5th ed., ed. D.W. Macdonald, et al., 634–639. Oxford: Oxford University Press.

Stierman, D.J. 8 June 1979. "Animals 'Hear' Quakes." *The San Bernardino County Sun*, 28.

Syrotuck, W.G. 1972. *Scent and the Scenting Dog*. Westmoreland, NY: Arner Publications.

Uexküll, J.v., and G. Kriszat. 1934. *Streifzüge durch die Umwelten von Tieren und Menschen*. Berlin: Verständliche Wissenschaft. http://dx.doi.org/10.1007/978-3-642-98976-6.

Vroon, P. 1989. *Zonder Geur Geen Emoties*. Amsterdam: De Volkskrant.

Wagner, K. 1930. *Rezente Hunderassen: Eine osteologische Untersuchung*. Oslo: J. Dybwad Publishers.

Wang, H.W., C.J. Wysocki, and G.H. Gold. 14 May 1993. "Induction of Olfactory Receptor Sensitivity in Mice." *Science* 260 (5110): 998–1000. http://dx.doi.org/10.1126/science.8493539.

Wedekind, C., and S. Furi. 1997. "Body Odour Preferences in Men and Women: Do They Aim for Specific MHC Combinations or Simply Heterozygosity?" *Proceedings of the Royal Society B: Biological Sciences*.http://dx.doi.org/10.1098/rspb.1997.0204.

Wilcox, R.M., and R.E. Johnston. 1995. "Scent Counter-Marks: Specialised Mechanisms of Perception and Response to Individual Odors in Golden Hamsters (*Mesocricetus auratus*)." *Journal of Comparative Psychology* 109 (4): 349–356. http://dx.doi.org/10.1037/0735-7036.109.4.349.

Yeshurun, Y., and N. Sobel. 2010. "An Odor Is Not Worth a Thousand Words: From Multidimensional Odors to Unidimensional Odor Objects." *Annual Review of Psychology* 61 (1): 219–241. http://dx.doi.org/10.1146/annurev.psych.60.110707.163639.

Youngentob, S.L., and P.F. Kent. 1995. "Enhancement of Odorant-Induced Mucosal Activity Patterns in Rats Trained on an Odorant Identification Task." *Brain Research* 670 (1): 82–88. http://dx.doi.org/10.1016/0006-8993(94)01275-M.

Zuschneid, K. 1973. "Die Riechleistung des Hundes." PhD diss., Berlin.

Additional Resources

Allison, A.C. May 1953. "The Morphology of the Olfactory System in the Vertebrates." *Biological Reviews of the Cambridge Philosophical Society* 28 (2): 195–244. http://dx.doi.org/10.1111/j.1469-185X.1953.tb01376.x.

Army Headquarters. 1977. *Military Police Working Dogs. Field Manual.* Washington, D.C.: U.S. Army.

Bernier, U.R., D.L. Kline, D.R. Barnard, C.E. Schreck, and R.A. Yost. 15 February 2000. "Analysis of Human Skin Emanations by Gas Chromatography/Mass Spectometry." *Analytical Chemistry* 72 (4): 747–756. http://dx.doi.org/10.1021/ac990963k.

Böttger, P. 1937. "Hunde im Dienste der Kriminalpolizei." *Zeitschrift für Hundeforschung.* Band V, 1–32.

Buytendijk, F.J.J. 1932. *De Psychologie van den Hond.* Amsterdam: Kosmos.

Catania, K.C. 21 December 2006. "Underwater 'Sniffing' by Semi-Aquatic Mammals." *Nature* 444 (7122): 1024–1025. http://dx.doi.org/10.1038/4441024a.

Catania, K.C., J.F. Hare, and K.L. Campbell. 15 January 2008. "Water Shrews Detect Movement, Shape, and Smell to Find Prey Underwater." *Proceedings of the National Academy of Sciences of the United States of America* 105 (2): 571–576. http://dx.doi.org/10.1073/pnas.0709534104.

Craven, B.A., E.G. Paterson, and G.S. Settles. 6 June 2010. "The Fluid Dynamics of Canine Olfaction: Unique Nasal Airflow Patterns as an Explanation of Macrosmia." *Journal of the Royal Society, Interface* 7 (47): 933–943. http://dx.doi.org/10.1098/rsif.2009.0490.

Ehrlichman, H., and L. Bastone. 1992. "The Use of Odour in the Study of Emotion." In *Fragrance: The Psychology and Biology of Perfume*, ed. S. Van Toller and G.H. Dodd. London: Springer.

———. 1992. "Olfaction and Emotion." In *Science of Olfaction*, ed. M. Serby and K. Chobor. New York: Springer. http://dx.doi.org/10.1007/978-1-4612-2836-3_15.

Ehrlichman, H., and J.N. Halpern. November 1988. "Affect and Memory: Effects of Pleasant and Unpleasant Odors on Retrieval of Happy and Unhappy

Memories." *Journal of Personality and Social Psychology* 55 (5): 769–779. http://dx.doi.org/10.1037/0022-3514.55.5.769.

Gerritsen, R., and R. Haak. 2001. *K9 Professional Tracking: A Complete Manual for Theory and Training*. Calgary: Detselig Enterprises.

———. 2013. *K9 Search and Rescue: Training the Natural Way*. Calgary: Brush Education Inc.

Gibbons, B. September 1986. "The Intimate Sense of Smell." *National Geographic*.

Grus, W.E. 2008. "Evolution of the Vomeronasal System Viewed through System-Specific Genes." PhD diss., University of Michigan.

Haak, R. 1984. *Het Africhten tot Verdedigingshond*. Best: Zuid Boekprodukties.

———. 1986. *Het Speuren van Honden in Theorie en Praktijk*. Best: Zuid Boekprodukties.

Hartman, D. 1991. *Honden Leren Sorteren en Speuren*. Best: Zuid Boekprodukties.

Hepper, P.G., and D.L. Wells. May 2005. "How Many Footsteps Do Dogs Need to Determine the Direction of an Odour Trail?" *Chemical Senses* 30 (4): 291–298. http://dx.doi.org/10.1093/chemse/bji023.

Horowitz, A. 2009. *Inside of a Dog: What Dogs See, Smell, and Know*. New York: Scribner.

Kaldenbach, J. 1997. *Police K-9: Organization and Management*. Almere.

———. 1998. *K9 Scent Detection*. Calgary: Detselig Enterprises, Ltd.

Lorenz, K. 1978. *Vergleichende Verhaltensforschung: Grundlagen der Ethologie*. Wien: Springer. http://dx.doi.org/10.1007/978-3-7091-3097-1.

Lundström, J.N., J.A. Boyle, R.J. Zatorre, and M. Jones-Gotman. August 2009. "The Neuronal Substrates of Human Olfactory-Based Kin Recognition." *Human Brain Mapping* 30 (8): 2571–2580. http://dx.doi.org/10.1002/hbm.20686.

Marples, E. January 1969. "Life on the Human Skin." *Scientific American* 220 (1): 108–115. http://dx.doi.org/10.1038/scientificamerican0169-108.

Matthes, E. 1926. "Die Physiologische Doppelnatur des Geruchsorganes der Urodelen im Hinblick auf seine Morphologische Zusammensetzung aus Haupthöhle und 'Jacobsonschem Organe.'" *Zeitschrife für vergleichende Physiologie* 4: 81–102.

Matthews, H.R., and J. Reisert. 15 September 2001. "Simultaneous Recording of Receptor Current and Intraciliary Ca2+ Concentration in Salamander Olfactory Receptor Cells." *Journal of Physiology* 535 (3): 637–645. http://dx.doi.org/10.1111/j.1469-7793.2001.00637.x.

———. August 2003. "Calcium: The Two-Faced Messenger of Olfactory Transduction and Adaptation." *Current Opinion in Neurobiology* 13 (4): 469–475. http://dx.doi.org/10.1016/S0959-4388(03)00097-7.

Menzel, R. and R. Menzel. 1930. *Die Verwertung der Riechfähigkeit des Hundes im Dienste der Menschheit*. Berlin: Kameradschaft-Verlag.

Moncrieff, R.W. October 1965. "Changes in Olfactory Preferences with Age." *Revue de Laryngologie - Otologie - Rhinologie* 86:895–904.

———. March 1954. "The Odorants." *Annals of the New York Academy of Sciences* 58 (2): 73–82. http://dx.doi.org/10.1111/j.1749-6632.1954.tb54846.x.

———. March 1957. "Olfactory Adaptation and Odor-Intensity." *American Journal of Psychology* 70 (1): 1–20. http://dx.doi.org/10.2307/1419225.

———. 1 October 1946. "The Sense of Smell." *Manufacturing Chemist and Aerosol News*.

———. 14 November 1957. "Variation of Odour Threshold Concentration with Percentage of Positive Responses." *Journal of Physiology* 139 (1): 10–14.

Most, K. 1926. "Neue Versuche über Spürfähigkeit." *Z.D. Hund* 18: 31–35.

———. 1977. *Training Dogs*. London: Popular Dogs.

Nagata, Y. 2003. "Measurement of Odor Threshold by Triangle Odor Bag Method." In *Odor Measurement Review*. Tokyo: Ministry of the Environment, Government of Japan.

Ochsenbein, U. 1979. *Der neue Weg der Hundeausbildung: Vom Gehorsamen Begleiter zum Dienst- und Rettungshund*. Rüschlikon-Zürich.

Pfungst, O. 1907. *Das Pferd des Herrn von Osten (Der kluge Hans): Ein Beitrag zur Experimentellen Tier- und Menschen-Psychologie*. Leipzig.

Pihlström, H. "The Size of Major Mammalian Sensory Organs as Measured from Cranial Characters, and Their Relation to the Biology and Evolution of Mammals." PhD diss., University of Helsinki, 2012.

Romanes, G.J. 21 July 1887. "Experiments on the Sense of Smell in Dogs." *Nature* 36 (925): 273–274. http://dx.doi.org/10.1038/036273a0.

Scheunert, A., and A. Trautmann. 1976. *Lehrbuch der Veterinärphysiologie*. Berlin: Paul Parey.

Schmidt, F. 1910. *Verbrecherspur und Polizeihund*. Augsburg, Germany: Springer Verlag.

Schoon, A., and R. Haak. 2002. *K9 Suspect Discrimination: Training and Practicing Scent Identification Line-Ups*. Calgary: Detselig Enterprises.

Seffrin, L. 1915. "Über die Kleinsten noch Wahrnehmbaren Geruchsmengen einiger Riechstoffe beim Hund." Z.f. Biol.

Seiferle, E. 1984. *Wesensgrundlagen und Wesensprüfung des Hundes*. Bern: Schweizerischen Kynologischen Gesellschaft.

Stoddart, D.M. 1980. *The Ecology of Vertebrate Olfaction*. London: Chapman and Hall. http://dx.doi.org/10.1007/978-94-009-5869-2.

Suárez, R., D. García-González, and F. de Castro. 24 December 2012. "Mutual Influences Between the Main Olfactory and Vomeronasal Systems in Development and Evolution." *Frontiers in Neuroanatomy* 6 (50).

Thesen, A., J.B. Steen, and K.B. Døving. 1993. "Behaviour of Dogs during Olfactory Tracking." *Journal of Experimental Biology* 180: 247–251.

Zelano, C., and N. Sobel. 3 November 2005. "Humans as an Animal Model for Systems-Level Organization of Olfaction." *Neuron* 48 (3): 431–454. http://dx.doi.org/10.1016/j.neuron.2005.10.009.

Zimen, E. 1978. *Der Wolf, Mythos und Verhalten*. Munich: Meyster Verlag.

———. 1988. *Der Hund, Abstammung, Verhalten, Mensch und Hund*. Munich: Bertelsmann.

About the Authors

Ruud Haak is the author of more than 30 dog books in Dutch and German. Since 1979 he has been the editor-in-chief of the biggest Dutch dog magazine, *Onze Hond (Our Dog)*. He was born in 1947 in Amsterdam, the Netherlands. At the age of 13, he was training police dogs at his uncle's security dog training center, and when he was 15 he worked after school with his patrol dog (which he trained himself) at the Amsterdam harbor. He later started training his dogs in Schutzhund and IPO and successfully bred and trained German shepherd dogs.

Ruud worked as a social therapist in a government clinic for criminal psychopaths. From his studies in psychology, he became interested in dog behavior and training methods for nose work, especially the tracking dog (Fährtenhund) and the search and rescue (SAR) dog. More recently he has trained drug and explosive detector dogs for the Dutch police and the Royal Dutch Airforce. He is also a visiting lecturer at Dutch, German, and Austrian police dog schools.

In the 1970s, Ruud and his wife, Dr. Resi Gerritsen, a psychologist and jurist, attended many courses and symposia with their German shepherds for Schutzhund, tracking dog, and SAR dog training in Switzerland, Germany, and Austria. In 1979

Ruud Haak and his dogs.

Dr. Resi Gerritsen and her dogs.

they started the Dutch Rescue Dog Organization in the Netherlands. With that unit, they attended many operations responding to earthquakes, gas explosions, and, of course, lost persons in large wooded or wilderness areas. In 1990 Ruud and Resi moved to Austria, where they were asked by the Austrian Red Cross to select and train operational SAR and avalanche dogs. They lived for three years at a height of six thousand feet (1800 m) in the Alps and worked with their dogs in many avalanche search missions.

With their Austrian colleagues, Ruud and Resi developed a new method for training SAR dogs. This way of training showed the best results after a major earthquake in Armenia (1988), and earthquakes in Japan (1995), Turkey (1999), and Algeria and Iran (2003), as well as many subsequent big earthquakes and other major events. Ruud and Resi have also demonstrated the success of their training methods at National and World Championships, where both were several times the leading champions.

Resi and Ruud have held many symposia and master classes all over the world on their unique training methods, which are featured in their books:

K9 Search and Rescue: Training the Natural Way

K9 Schutzhund Training: A Manual for IPO Training through Positive Reinforcement

K9 Professional Tracking: A Complete Manual for Theory and Training

K9 Personal Protection: A Manual for Training Reliable Protection Dogs.

K9 Complete Care: A Manual for Physically and Mentally Healthy Working Dogs

K9 Working Breeds: Characteristics and Capabilities

K9 Fraud: Fraudulent Handling of Police Dogs

With Simon Prins they wrote *K9 Behavior Basics: A Manual for Proven Success in Operational Service Dog Training*; and with Dr. Adee Schoon, Ruud wrote *K9 Suspect Discrimination: Training and Practicing Scent Identification Line-ups*. All of these books were published by Detselig Enterprises in Calgary, Canada (now Brush Education Inc.).

Ruud and Resi now live in the Netherlands. They are training directors and international judges for the International Red Cross

Federation, the United Nations (OCHA), the International Rescue Dog Organisation (IRO), and the Fédération Cynologique Internationale (FCI).

At the moment Ruud and Resi are still successfully training their dogs as detector dogs for SAR, drugs, explosives, and in IPO and protection dog training. You can contact the authors by e-mail at: onzehond@bcm.nl.